TARGETING THE TRENDSETTING CONSUMER

HOW TO MARKET YOUR PRODUCT OR SERVICE TO INFLUENTIAL BUYERS

Irma Zandl
Richard Leonard

BUSINESS ONE IRWIN
Homewood, Illinois 60430

This publication is designed to provide accurate and authoritative information in regard to the subject matter covered. It is sold with the understanding that neither the author nor the publisher is engaged in rendering legal, accounting, or other professional service. If legal advice or other expert assistance is required, the services of a competent professional should be sought.

From a Declaration of Principles jointly adopted by a Committee of the American Bar Association and a Committee of Publishers.

Sponsoring editor: Cynthia A. Zigmund
Project editor: Jane Lightell
Production manager: Diane Palmer
Jacket Designer: Sam Concialdi
Compositor: Impressions, a Division of Edwards Brothers, Inc.
Typeface: 11/13 Century Schoolbook
Printer: R. R. Donnelley & Sons Company

Library of Congress Cataloging-in-Publication Data

Zandl, Irma.
    Targeting the trendsetting consumer : how to market your product or service to influential buyers / Irma Zandl, Richard Leonard.
       p.   cm.
    ISBN 1-55623-478-3
    1. Consumer behavior. 2. Motivation research (Marketing) 3. Marketing. I. Leonard, Richard (Richard H.) II. Title.
HF5415.32.Z36 1992
658.8′34—dc20   91-31261

Printed in the United States of America
1 2 3 4 5 6 7 8 9 0 DOC 8 7 6 5 4 3 2 1

CONTENTS

Preface   vii

PART I
UNDERSTANDING THE
TRENDSETTING CONSUMER

1	Who Are They?	1
2	Why Are They Important?	10
3	Purchase Behavior	14
4	Monitoring the Trendsetters	28

PART II
CASE HISTORIES

5	Long-Term Successes	45
6	Evolutionary Successes	55
7	Repositioning Successes	62
8	Reverse-Chic Successes	73
9	Too-Soon-to-Tell Successes	75
10	Short-Term Successes	86
11	Missed Opportunities	92

PART III
MARKETING GUIDELINES

12	Strategic Planning	103
13	Semiotics	111
14	Visual Design	116
15	Distribution and Location	125
16	Customer Service	131
17	Direct Marketing	137

18	Public Relations	143
19	Advertising	155
20	Promotion	169
21	Green Marketing	179

Checklist 187

Closing Thoughts 193

Notes 195

Index 207

PREFACE

Our involvement with trendsetting consumers is an outgrowth of our marketing consulting business, which includes trend forecasting, strategic planning, creative marketing, and promotion. In forecasting trends for our clients in a broad range of products and services, we discovered an elusive group of consumers who instinctively initiate the trends that everyone else will follow. These people—whom we call *Alphas*—are the subject of this book. Although their number is limited, their influence is vast.

Unlike mainstream consumers, Alphas are unafraid to be the first. To do it. Buy it. Eat it. Wear it. In that sense, they are the dream consumers of anyone with something new to sell. Indeed, they often represent a critical step in starting a purchase cycle. But their influence extends to existing businesses as well because many mainstream consumers take their purchase cues from the Alphas: without the endorsement of the Alpha consumer it is often impossible to achieve mainstream acceptance—the kind of acceptance associated with market share, economies of scale, and impressive profit margins.

Alphas are trendsetting consumers but they are not "trendoids"—those consumers in eternal pursuit of the new. Alpha's independence and sense of self-direction tend to make them impervious to fads, which increases their importance to marketers with a long-term perspective. When the performance of a product or service is satisfactory, Alphas are very brand loyal; this brand loyalty can be a critical factor in maintaining a desirable image for your business in the eyes of the mainstream consumer.

Many marketing and advertising executives today recognize the importance of Alpha consumers in their industries but do not know how to target them for business development; this book was written in direct response to their needs. The reader will learn how to identify, understand, and successfully reach these influential buyers; and the book has been organized to provide an easy source for future reference with chapters on specific marketing functions, from strategic planning to promotion.

APPROACH

We have analyzed Alpha consumers individually and collectively to determine their purchase behaviors. We looked at the products and services they buy in a variety of industries—from toothpaste to nightclubs—to identify common elements. And we explored their responses to specific marketing strategies that have been employed in the past, including advertising, public relations, direct marketing, and promotional programs, to generate guidelines for businesses targeting the Alpha consumer. At first glance, Chanel and Harley-Davidson—two brands that enjoy a fanatical degree of brand loyalty among Alpha consumers—may appear to be worlds apart, but upon closer examination we discovered some very fundamental similarities, similarities that should prove instructive to anyone targeting the Alpha consumer. We have confined our study to the U.S. market in the last decade and interviewed a number of the professionals associated with significant marketing successes of those years to gain insight into their strategic perspectives on the 1980s and their outlook for the 1990s.

HOW TO USE THIS BOOK

The book includes three parts:

Part I: Understanding the Trendsetting Consumer

Chapters 1 through 4 focus on Alpha consumers: their sensibilities, values, and purchase behaviors; their influence on mainstream consumers and the diffusion of trends; and ways to monitor Alphas in the 1990s so that you can plan your marketing strategy accordingly.

Part II: Case Histories

Chapters 5 through 11 include historical examples of products and services that appealed to Alphas in the last decade with implications for marketers today. The chapters have been organized according to several general marketing scenarios, such as Long-Term Successes, Evolutionary Successes, and Reverse-Chic Successes, to illustrate common success factors.

Part III: Marketing Guidelines

Based on the psychographic profile of the Alpha consumer that emerged and the lessons learned from the case histories, chapters 12 through 21 provide general marketing guidelines for targeting this consumer, with separate chapters on Strategic Planning, Semiotics, Visual Design, Distribution and Location, Customer Service, Direct Marketing, Public Relations, Advertising, Promotion, and Green Marketing.

PART I

UNDERSTANDING THE TRENDSETTING CONSUMER

A thorough understanding of the trendsetting consumer should be the foundation for your marketing strategy, because ultimately it is this consumer who will determine whether you succeed or fail. In Part I, we explore the common characteristics of Alpha consumers—their values, interests, and sensibilities—to provide clues to their purchase behaviors. These fundamental values should inform every aspect of your marketing strategy, from corporate identity to promotion, to develop the type of emotional bond with these consumers that translates into brand loyalty.

We also examine the role of the Alpha consumer in the marketplace, including the initiation and diffusion of trends, starting a purchase cycle, and maintaining a desirable brand identity in the eyes of the mainstream who often take their purchase cues from these influential buyers. We address some of the implications for new products or services; for existing businesses; for widely distributed products, such as consumer packaged goods; and for businesses with a narrow customer base, such as restaurants. And we identify some of the economic factors you should consider, including trade policies, distribution, advertising, and promotional programs and profitability.

Finally, we provide suggestions for monitoring Alpha consumers in the 1990s to help you anticipate their influence on your business. Our methodology ranges from reading trade publications in seemingly disparate industries to closely following the activities of prophetic Alphas with established track records, whether they are public personalities, like Jane Fonda, or marketing professionals, like Ian Schrager.

We have included a variety of products and services in our discussion to provide you with a broad frame of reference, but you will have to interpret the information within the context of your business.

CHAPTER 1

WHO ARE THEY?

Alpha consumers are resistant to easy categorization because they can be found throughout the country. In every market, every product category, every social group regardless of its size, there is always someone who is the first to buy the latest development in home electronics. Wear a new style of clothing. Try a new shampoo. Go to a new restaurant. Discover a new travel destination. In many respects the Alphas mirror the general population. Age, sex, ethnic background, religion, marital status, and geographical locations are not distinguishing factors. However, there is a distinct Alpha sensibility that sets these consumers apart from the mainstream, who generally lack the inclination and self-assurance to be pioneers. For example, Alphas frequently choose to live in neighborhoods that are considered "transitional" or "up-and-coming," such as the East Village in Manhattan, the Flats in Cleveland, or the SoMa district in San Francisco. Their motivations may vary—an insolvent artist may be seeking inexpensive studio space whereas an affluent lawyer may be attracted by the relative solitude of underdeveloped areas—but each has chosen to be a pioneer.

Everyone knows at least a few Alpha consumers; we will look at two. Although their demographic profiles and interests are different, each possesses a distinctive Alpha sensibility that sets him or her apart from the crowd.

Elizabeth*, age 32, lives in a loft in Manhattan's bohemian East Village with her husband and two-year-old daughter. Al-

*pseudonym

though she grew up on the tony Upper East Side and attended the Spence School, an exclusive private school for girls, Elizabeth has lived "downtown" ever since she graduated from the Harvard Business School: "I feel really strongly about the lower East Side. I love the sense of community, all the inexpensive and fun restaurants, the ethnic variety of people, all the different little stores. . . . By now I'm almost committed to never leave my neighborhood." She has her hair cut in the neighborhood at the ultrahip and inexpensive Astor Place Barber Shop, but she is willing to venture uptown to the Bronx to Loehmann's discount clothing store in search of mark-downs on her favorite designer, Geoffrey Beene.

Elizabeth's education and career reflect the diversity of her interests. After majoring in philosophy at Harvard College, she tried to get a job in the fashion industry, "but it's hard for a shiksa from Harvard to a get a job on Seventh Avenue," so she

ASTOR PLACE BARBER SHOP IN NEW YORK
Clients for the $10.00 haircuts range from East Village Punks and Kids from Brooklyn to Harry Connick, Jr. and John Kennedy, Jr.

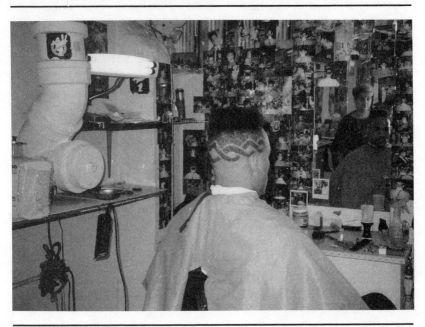

went to work for the investment banking firm of Morgan Stanley. After two years on Wall Street, she decided to return to Harvard to get her MBA. She then pursued her original interest in fashion: "I was always very entrepreneurial. . . . Somehow I got it in my mind that I could start this dress company." The result was a venture designed to provide professional women with stylish alternatives to the dress-for-success, floppy-bow-tie, and men's-style-suit look that was prevalent at the time. After some initial success, she ran into production and financial problems—and returned to the world of investment banking. In 1987 "before the Crash," she again went out on her own as a consultant and writer; her projects have ranged from advising Oliver Stone on the production of his *Wall Street* film to serving as an interim CEO for a magazine. On her career: "What I'm striving for in my life is no real difference between my work and my life—or at least be doing something that I really enjoy doing."

Elizabeth is married to a painter and very involved in the art world. She reads a lot (*Vanity Fair* is her favorite magazine) and would read even more "if I had the time." She has found that motherhood has made her more domestic: She now cooks, gardens on the fire escape, and tries to spend more evenings at home with her daughter. She does not watch television, but she loves movies, from classics like *The Women* to recent films, like *sex, lies and videotape*. She is very eco-aware and tries to buy products that are "environmentally friendly," such as Origins Skincare at Bergdorf Goodman and things from "The Seventh Generation" mail order catalog. Elizabeth's definition of hip: "On the edge yet totally one's own."

David, age 47, also decided to pursue an entrepreneurial vision after many years of corporate experience in brand management and advertising account management. Two years ago, he started his own marketing and sales promotion firm in New York. He feels the rewards far outweigh the risks of self-employment: "You have a great deal of freedom—you're only answerable to yourself." David grew up in Providence, Rhode Island, went to the University of Rhode Island, and got his MBA from New York University—and has lived in New York ever since.

After 25 years, David has ambivalent feelings about life in

New York City. He loves "the stimulation . . . generally things happen first here . . . people seem a little sharper—I don't know that they're necessarily smarter—but they're sharper," and he takes full advantage of the city's restaurants (The Gotham is his favorite), stores (he likes to buy Giorgio Armani clothes at Barneys), and cultural institutions (he visits the Metropolitan Museum most frequently). He enjoys living in Tribeca, an industrial area that is gradually becoming more residential, because "it's sort of like being in the country . . . you're removed from New York yet close to the Village and Soho . . . on the weekends, there's very little traffic, so it's easy to get around, easy to park." (In the summer, David usually escapes to a beach house in the Hamptons that he rents with a group of friends.) On the other hand, he feels that the quality of life in New York is declining and is considering moving to Los Angeles or San Francisco.

An affluent bachelor, David is a very discriminating consumer, particularly when electronics, financial services, or travel are involved. And, as a marketing and advertising professional, he has a heightened sense of awareness of new developments in the marketplace. David's definition of hip: "Someone who knows how to act in any situation."

Elizabeth and David share common values that shape their lives—and purchase behaviors. Individuals are often complex, and Alphas are no exception, but all of them possess to varying degrees the fundamental traits that characterize the Alpha consumer. Common Alpha values include:

Information

Alpha consumers are very well informed and place a great deal of importance on knowledge. This generally motivates them to pursue a high level of formal education throughout their lives; education does not end with college or graduate school for most Alphas, who continue to take courses in everything from early music and financial investing to photography and bridge. It also makes Alphas voracious readers—everything from newspapers to the most esoteric magazines, from best-selling authors to the most obscure novelist. Their quest for knowledge also leads them to identify the best-informed people in their immediate world, who then become important sources of information.

Cosmopolitanism

Alphas like to know many people from different worlds—from various professional, social, and geographical worlds—because it increases their sources of information. Most Alphas move easily from one world to another, which fosters a broad range of interests and a very cosmopolitan outlook; they are extremely receptive to the new and the different. This is reflected in their travel destinations, which are usually foreign and frequently off the beaten track.

Communication

Interpersonal communication involving the exchange of ideas and information is extremely important to Alphas and tends to make them very social creatures. Alphas go out frequently with other people—to restaurants, clubs, cultural institutions, concerts, and sports events—and they are avid users of the telephone (including long-distance, which enables them to be plugged-in to their personal network of information sources at all times). The emphasis on interpersonal communication also makes many Alphas articulate and engaging company, which increases their popularity and influence.

Originality

Alphas value originality and independence. Their knowledge of history and popular culture enables them to recognize authenticity, and they have a general disdain for imitation in everything from the arts to consumer products. However, they also appreciate an element of surprise or unpredictability, which is frequently reflected in their penchant for iconoclasm—classics that are playfully twisted. Not surprisingly, Alphas are easily bored and avoid the routine in their choice of careers, hobbies, recreation, and entertainment. This often leads them in creative directions professionally where they can pursue their independent vision; for example, Alphas are more likely to be found in the free-wheeling worlds of fashion and entertainment than in more circumscribed fields. Alphas are frequently involved in the arts where originality is perhaps most highly valued; many Alphas are writers, artists, photographers, musicians, and performers, either by profession or avocation, and they are regular patrons of museums, galleries, theater, dance, and musical performances.

Involvement

Although their individual interests may vary, all Alphas are obsessive about certain things. Their passionate involvement with their careers, hobbies, or social causes often propels them to high levels of achievement. This in turn enhances their stature among other consumers; everyone admires accomplished and successful people. And the professional achievements of Alphas frequently result in the financial success that enables them to be pioneering consumers in high-ticket categories like automobiles, electronics, travel, and luxury goods.

Identity

Alphas have a very strong sense of self-identity, which provides them with the motivation—and confidence—to follow their singular vision regardless of the crowd. Unlike mainstream consumers, whose primary motivation is peer acceptance, Alphas are unconcerned with popular opinion. Indeed, many Alphas derive a certain pleasure in standing out from the crowd and they respect others—individuals, businesses, and institutions—who follow a distinctive vision. Accordingly, Alphas value integrity and are extremely sensitive to inconsistency, lack of conviction, and hypocrisy. For example, the active role in environmental protection that has been assumed by the Aveda Corporation of Minneapolis and its chairman, Horst Rechelbacher—from recycling programs for its customers to Earth Day sponsorship—has enhanced the appeal of its haircare and beauty products formulated with natural ingredients for consumers with a green orientation. The company's corporate policies are consistent with its product.

Self-Sufficiency

With their broad knowledge, acute social intelligence, activist nature, and strong sense of self-identity, it is not surprising that Alphas demand a great deal of control over their destiny. They do not wait for others to provide direction, and they often resent being told what they should do (or buy). They are the first to investigate alternative approaches to enhance their sense of control; they often circumvent obstacles that the crowd may haplessly accept—and they admire others who do the same. This questioning of the status quo occasionally makes Alphas appear to be renegades, which contributes to their hip status in the eyes of other consumers.

These critical values inform everything Alphas do. Businesses targeting Alpha consumers should keep these values in mind when developing their marketing strategies; psychographics are clearly more significant than demographics in targeting these influential buyers. In the next chapter we address the importance of Alpha consumers in the marketplace and their influence on the purchase behavior of the mainstream, and we will look at some historical examples.

CHAPTER 2

WHY ARE THEY IMPORTANT?

Based on the consumer research that we have conducted through-out the country in the last 5 years, including observational research, shopping mall intercepts, focus groups, and mail-in questionnaires, and our experience in trend forecasting, we believe that about 1 in 20 consumers is an Alpha. Their distinctive sensibility is innate; it does not change—and it cannot be acquired. Although many Alphas gravitate to urban centers where there are more opportunities to pursue their professional and avocational interests, they may be found in every community and social group regardless of its size because there is always someone who is the first to test a new product or service. The timing of the initial purchase may vary because trends evolve at different rates throughout the country, but the market dynamics are the same.

Despite their limited number, Alphas wield a tremendous amount of power in the marketplace. Since they are usually the first to test a new product or service, it is often impossible to start a purchase cycle without them. Moreover, businesses must successfully reach a significant percentage of Alpha consumers during the initial sales period to generate the perception of success that is critical to building trade support and attracting the mainstream. For this reason, manufacturers targeting Alpha consumers may want to limit initial product distribution to a few stores in markets where there is a relatively large Alpha population. Estée Lauder Inc., with annual sales of about $2.3 billion,[1] is the most powerful company in the $5-billion U.S. prestige cosmetics industry. (In addition to the Estée Lauder brand, the company manufactures the Clinique, Prescriptives, and Aramis products.) When Estée Lauder introduced Origins Natural Resources in 1990, a line of skincare, makeup, and sensory therapy with a New Age positioning designed to appeal to the Alpha consumer, distribution was limited to Bergdorf Goodman in New York City and selected Nordstrom stores in California. Although the parent company easily could have compelled every department store in the country to carry the Origins line, it recognized that the perception of immediate success in two influential retail stores in trendsetting markets would be a critical factor in building a base for long-term growth and expanded distribution.

There is also a strong economic argument to support targeted Alpha marketing during the introductory phase: Because Alphas are less responsive to major advertising campaigns and expensive sales promotion techniques than the average consumer (see chapter 3, Purchase Behavior), heavy investment spending is not required at this point, affording companies the opportunity to gradually achieve the volume that can profitably support big promotional budgets.

Not only are Alphas the first to test a new product or service, they also frequently pioneer new ways of consumption that can lead to new marketing strategies involving everything from product positioning to line extensions and new products. In a similar way, the Alpha consumer often pioneers new methods of purchase. For example, Alphas were at the vanguard of the movement in this country away from general merchandise stores, like department stores, toward specialty retailing. Many Alpha consumers had been exposed to this approach on their foreign travels, particularly in countries like France, where even the most prosaic product is artfully merchandised. At the same time, Alphas' quest for unique products and stores with a distinct point of view caused them to become increasingly dissatisfied with the general merchandise stores, many of which were indistinguishable from each other. Alpha consumers enthusiastically embraced the specialty stores, from discount electronics chains to exclusive one-of-a-kind boutiques.

Alphas influence other consumers in two primary ways. First, Alphas are usually great communicators. As we observed in chapter 1, they value the exchange of information with others—and they make the results of their purchase experiments widely known. They are generally articulate, opinionated, and well-informed, so their recommendation—or rejection—can strongly influence the purchase intent of other consumers. Indeed, many people actively seek the advice of the Alpha consumer, particularly in an industry or product category where they feel uninformed. Common examples include technical products, like automobiles and electronics, travel destinations, hotels, clubs, restaurants, fashion, and myriad services—everything from haircuts to financial planning.

Second, Alphas shape the aspirations of the mainstream, who have few role models today. The new scrutiny in the media of anyone in the public eye, from politicians and business leaders to film stars and professional athletes, has left many consumers with few heroes. These people lack the self-direction Alphas possess and frequently look to them for direction. In addition to their knowledge and self-assurance, Alphas tend to be charismatic and hip, cynosures wherever they go, which considerably enhances their authority. Even the implicit endorsement of an Alpha consumer—driving a certain car, drinking a certain liquor, dining in a certain restaurant—contributes immeasurably to a product's desirability among the mainstream. Indeed, savvy marketers should look upon their Alpha customers as de facto press agents for their businesses.

The influence of the Alpha consumer is growing because the mainstream consumer has become increasingly sophisticated and cynical. In recent years, all of the illogical celebrity endorsements, misleading product claims, and specious corporate philanthropy have undermined the credibility of traditional marketing programs. Today, it is word-of-mouth and personal exposure that drives sales; Alpha consumers are considered objective and unbiased sources of information—and they make known their opinions.

In some categories the Alpha consumer is often professionally involved in the industry. In the fashion industry, for example, the professionals—the editors, stylists, photographers, models, retailers, and visual display designers—are critical. Many of these people travel to the fashion capitals of the world on a regular basis—for the seasonal collections, for example—where they are exposed, not only to the latest runway fashions but also, equally important, to the local street fashions, which can be far more directional. This informs their personal style and professional judgments, which in turn can make or break a manufacturer; without stylish editorial coverage and appropriate retail distribution and merchandising, an apparel manufacturer is unlikely to succeed. In other categories the Alpha consumer tends to operate outside the establishment. For example, in popular music— from Harlem in the 1920s to rock and roll in the 1950s to Motown in the 1960s to rap in the 1980s—blacks have set the pace independently of the music industry. But whatever the profile of the Alpha consumer in your business, you ignore this influential buyer at your own peril.

CHAPTER 3

PURCHASE BEHAVIOR

The purchase behavior of the Alpha consumer is guided by the common values outlined in chapter 1:

- information
- cosmopolitanism
- communication
- originality
- involvement
- identity
- self-sufficiency

As with any other consumer, the purchase behavior of the Alpha consumer is influenced by contemporary social conditions as well; the Alpha consumer may be more independent, but he or she is also a member of society. In the 1980s, for example, Alpha consumers were as involved with "designer" brands as mainstream consumers were, but the perspective was quite different. Alphas appreciated the aspect of originality and the distinctive identity that many designer brands represented; for the mainstream, these products were aspirational purchases that symbolized status and social acceptance. The common values shared by the Alpha consumer are timeless—like the inherent sensibility that distinguishes these consumers—but these values must be interpreted within the context of contemporary society.

INFORMATION

The Alpha's pursuit of knowledge makes her or him a very inquisitive, informed, and discriminating consumer. Alphas never stop conducting their own independent research. Sometimes this research is deliberate following a decision to buy a new car or stereo system, take a vacation, or find a new haircutter. Other times this research is subconscious, the result of the Alpha's general quest for information, which is manifested in reading, social exchanges, and heightened awareness of new developments in the marketplace.

For the Alpha consumer, the most important sources of information include other consumers whose judgments are respected and trusted. This is usually another Alpha. A positive recommendation from someone perceived as an objective and disinterested party is often cited as motivation to investigate a new product or service; Alphas feel that it has then been "screened" or "field-tested" for them personally. Conversely, a negative review can discourage further investigation.

Critical reviews by professionals and editorial coverage are also important sources of information when the reviewer's integrity and perceived objectivity is respected. Alphas know when the source is biased or has a vested interest—for example, they realize that a magazine's advertisers generally receive favorable editorial coverage—and they selectively synthesize this information. As with their personal contacts, Alphas identify the most valuable sources of information in the media and follow them closely, whether it is George Wayne's coverage of the club scene in *Paper*, Terrence Rafferty's film reviews in *The New Yorker*, or Jane Bryant Quinn's financial planning advice in *Newsweek*.

Alpha purchase behavior is influenced by knowledge of the company and its management as well as the quality of the actual product or service. Some of this information is public. Alphas are cognizant of a company's heritage, subsidiaries, social and environmental policies, and philanthropy from their highly eclectic media consumption. Some of this information is not public; Alphas have a wide network of personal contacts and are frequently privy to inside information, which enables them to read "between-the-lines." Like the girl who "danced with a boy who danced with a girl who danced with the Prince of Wales," Alphas often have their own channels of information, however tangential.

Alphas selectively utilize the information presented in marketing and sales programs, including advertising, promotional literature, labeling and package copy, and salespeople. They appreciate direct product information and reject obvious sales techniques, from celebrity endorsements to premiums to sycophantic salespeople. In some cases, the Alpha consumer will seek the recommendation of a professional with expertise, such as a knowledgeable sommelier, travel agent, interior decorator, or hairstylist. In general, however, Alpha consumers prefer to make purchase decisions independently once they feel that they have obtained the necessary information.

The Alpha's quest for information leads to a recognition and appreciation of quality, which is most often cited as the greatest determinant in purchase motivation and brand loyalty. And Alphas are willing to pay a premium for quality. For example, the Alpha consumer would pay $800 for a Marcel Breuer chair (the classic chair with a tubular-steel frame and a caned seat and back designed by the great architect in the 1920s) at the Knoll Group with whom Breuer signed a contract, although there are ubiquitous knockoffs available that range in price from $45 at the Door Store to $300 at Palazzetti, all of which look the same to the average person. This does not mean, however, that Alphas do not seek value. There are Alpha women, for example, who know that Cosmair Inc. markets two lines of cosmetics in this country (Lancôme at a premium price-point in department stores and L'Oréal at a moderate price-point in drug stores), have tried both brands' mascaras, ascertained that they were of comparable quality (if not identical), and opted for L'Oréal because it represents the greater value. Alphas appreciate a "deal" as much as other consumers, but they will seldom compromise on quality.

COSMOPOLITANISM

The Alpha consumer's cosmopolitan outlook exposes him or her to a broader range of goods and services than the average consumer. This encourages trial and experimentation, which makes the Alpha consumer particularly receptive to new products. Sometimes the new product represents a genuine innovation within its category; other times it represents new distribution of an imported product or service. Alphas frequently embrace things they first "discovered" on their foreign travels, from Perrier to Shiatsu, when they become available locally. And they often have a preference for imported goods, due in part to the perception of superior quality, in part to the product's foreign heritage.

This cosmopolitan point of view also influences the nature of Alpha brand loyalty. Alphas are brand loyal but often to a stable of brands within a category. They frequently have a collector's mentality; one might find five kinds of mustard in the refrigerator or 30 pairs of shoes in the closet or 1,000 books in the den, but in each case the consumer enjoys the process of collecting, editing, and increasing his or her consumption options.

COMMUNICATION

Alphas are very conscious of the message conveyed by a product's positioning, heritage, design, packaging, merchandising, distribution, advertising, and promotion. In much the same way that Alphas value interpersonal communication involving the exchange of ideas and information, they appreciate products and services that clearly convey differentiation. And just as Alphas often enjoy standing out from the crowd, they respect goods and services that are in some way unique or different from the competition. Differentiation may be communicated in various ways. For example, Alphas are generally literate and articulate, which makes them very sensitive to copy; they respond favorably to a concise communication of product benefits, comprehensive product description, appropriate literary allusions, and humor (particularly British humor with its tradition of puns and intricate wordplay). At the same time, Alphas' involvement, whether by profession or avocation, in such highly visual fields as art, architecture, interior design, fashion, visual merchandising, graphic design, and film enhances their appreciation of visual style and energy in everything from packaging to restaurant design. They are also very cognizant of more subtle semiotics, such as location and distribution. For example, Wolfgang Puck's decision to locate his restaurant Eureka on the outskirts of Los

Angeles in a cinder-block building that looks like a factory without signage contributes to its "insider's cachet." Similarly, Paul Mitchell's decision to limit distribution of their haircare products to salons despite the easy temptation to sell to retail stores enhances their mystique. The summation of these messages equals the product's identity in the mind of the Alpha consumer. In building brand loyalty and repeat purchase, a distinctive identity and positioning is second in importance only to the perception of quality.

ORIGINALITY

The Alpha respect for originality is manifested in two distinct ways: a recognition and appreciation of authenticity and of innovation. Authenticity is a key factor in the enduring appeal of such diverse goods and services as Levi jeans, Kellogg Corn Flakes, Harley-Davidson, American Express, the Ritz Bar in Paris, and the Four Seasons Restaurant in New York—all of which are perceived as "originals" or "classics" within their categories. The emphasis on authenticity frequently leads to a disdain for products considered imitations, something any marketer considering competitive advertising should keep in mind because it automatically places the sponsor in a defensive "me-too" posture. An Alpha cola drinker, for example, is more likely to choose Coke over Pepsi, due in no small part to years of comparison advertising from Pepsi.

INVOLVEMENT

As in the other aspects of their lives, such as their careers, hobbies, and social causes, Alphas are very involved consumers. They recognize quality and demand product satisfaction. When a product or service performs satisfactorily, they are very brand loyal. Their expectations are not unrealistic, however; they are seldom swayed by extravagant and unbelievable promises. On the other hand, when a product or service fails to deliver satisfaction, the activist nature of Alpha consumers becomes very apparent: Not only will they discontinue patronage, they are likely to actively express their dissatisfaction by refusing to pay (or demanding a refund), registering complaints with owners or senior management, notifying consumer protection agencies, and perhaps most important, advising their acquaintances to boycott the establishment or product as well.

Alpha involvement extends beyond the quality of the actual product or service to its ownership or management. As we noted, Alphas frequently possess information—sometimes public, sometimes private—about a company's management, social and environmental policies, and philanthropy, and they seek establishments that share their values. For example, Alphas with a heightened sense of social responsibility may refuse to purchase products from a manufacturer with a harmful environmental record. On the other hand, Alphas with a concern for education will be favorably predisposed toward companies that support schools and universities in their philanthropic programs.

Finally, Alphas' involvement with other pursuits tends to make them very deliberate consumers. Purchase is often considered a mission—even a chore. The Alpha consumer seldom shops for fun or adventure; there are simply too many other things she or he would rather do. This presents both advantages and disadvantages to businesses targeting this consumer: It contributes significantly to brand loyalty because Alphas do not like to waste time shopping or searching for a new restaurant or dry cleaner or stock broker; repurchase saves time and energy. But it also requires fanatical attention to detail on the part of businesses targeting this consumer. To attract and retain their patronage, businesses must enhance Alpha consumers' experiences with superior product quality and selection, exemplary service, a distinctive ambience, and an element of entertainment (which might be anything from visual excitement to an interesting clientele).

IDENTITY

The strong sense of self-identity that provides Alpha consumers with the motivation and confidence to follow their singular vision regardless of the crowd leads to a genuine respect for products and businesses that possess a distinct identity or brand image.

The creation of a clearly defined identity with product differentiation is an essential factor in generating trial and is second in importance only to perceived product quality in stimulating repeat purchase and building brand loyalty. The establishment of an affinity or emotional bond between the consumer and your product or business is always desirable; with the Alpha consumer it is absolutely imperative. Unlike the mainstream consumer, who is more susceptible to peer pressure and more responsive to short-term marketing and sales approaches, from discounting to sweepstakes to premiums, the Alpha consumer will not patronize a business he or she does not esteem. The presentation of a consistent, clearly defined brand image is the first step in developing this esteem.

Product identity is created in many different ways. We have noted how Alphas' pursuit of information contributes to their knowledge of a company and its management and social policies as well as its products or services. Although the Alpha consumer may respond favorably to the company's overt marketing program—everything from product design to advertising—he or she will not separate it from its origins. Its corporate heritage becomes an intrinsic part of its identity. For example, under the dynamic leadership of Geraldine Stutz, Henri Bendel in New York was a unique specialty clothing store favored by many Alpha women. When the store was acquired by the Limited (known for its mass market clothing chains, including the Limited, Victoria's Secret, Lerner's, and Lane Bryant) and managed from the Limited corporate offices in Columbus, Ohio, it lost its allure for the Alpha consumer, not to mention Henri Bendel, the 83-year-old nephew of the store's founder, who was conspicuously absent from the lavish festivities when the new Henri Bendel store in New York opened on Fifth Avenue in 1991. ("I guess it might have been embarrassing to them," said Mr. Bendel. "I stand for something, and they stand for something else."[1])

We have also noted how the Alpha interest in communication leads to a heightened awareness of semiotics; everything a company does sends a message that becomes part of its identity in the mind of the Alpha consumer. Salespeople, for example, should reflect the company's philosophy in their knowledge and involvement with the product, their sales approach, and their appearance. In a bookstore, literate "odd-balls" with a genuine passion for books may be the most effective salespeople while hip young club kids may be more appropriate in a clothing boutique, but in either case, they send a distinct signal to the consumer.

Although Alphas recognize and respect originality and independence, in the long run, the perception of integrity and consistency is more important than an iconoclastic vision in building consumer esteem. For example, Alpha consumers who had admired some of director David Lynch's quirky early films, like *Eraserhead* and *The Elephant Man*, eagerly awaited his television debut with the "Twin Peaks" series, which they watched when it premiered in the spring of 1990, contributing significantly to the "buzz" it created and its initial success in the ratings. However, when it became clear that the program was self-consciously unorthodox, the Alpha viewer immediately lost interest—and the rest of the audience followed. (The show was soon canceled.)

Finally, although it's difficult to analyze—and even more difficult to create—mystique is a fundamental element in the development of a desirable brand identity. It is often a product's mystique that attracts and maintains the interest of the Alpha consumer. Sometimes mystique is the result of an insider's cachet created by positive word-of-mouth; this is often the case with singular establishments, such as restaurants, nightclubs, and hotels. Sometimes it is the result of exclusivity where limited distribution, high price-points, or restricted membership (or "door") policies may prevent the masses from ever becoming customers. Sometimes it is the result of unique advertising; for example, in the 1980s, the distinctive campaigns created for Absolut vodka by TBWA, Inc.; for Nike by Weiden & Kennedy; and for Calvin Klein's Obsession fragrances by Richard Avedon, Doon Arbus, and Bruce Weber contributed significantly to their mystique. Sometimes mystique is the result of a product's heritage; over the years Coca-Cola, Levi jeans, Harley-Davidson motorcycles, and Marlboro cigarettes have become American icons with undeniable mystique throughout the world. Sometimes it is the result of the individuals directly involved with the creation of the product: Ben Cohen and Jerry Greenfield, the founders of Ben & Jerry's Ice Cream; Tina Brown, the editor of *Vanity Fair*; Wolfgang Puck, the owner of the Spago, Chinois, Postrio, Eureka, and Granita restaurants in California; and Paloma Picasso, the creative force behind various products that bear her signature, from jewelry at Tiffany to perfume at Cosmair, are integral parts of their business's mystique. More often than not, however, mystique is the intangible benefit of a clear sense of self-identity: knowing who you are and who your customers are; following your own vision instead of reacting to your competitors; and not attempting to be all things to all people, which usually ends up satisfying no one.

SELF-SUFFICIENCY

Alphas are by nature highly self-sufficient. As consumers, they generally like to control the purchase process and frequently resent the intrusion of unsolicited marketing techniques, from advertising to aggressive salespeople. This presents a distinct challenge to marketers and advertisers. For example, many Alphas have unlisted telephone numbers (and others often utilize the "call-screening" features of their answering machines), which makes telemarketing difficult. And, faced with proliferating junk mail, Alphas are increasingly asking agencies, like the Mail Preference Service of the Direct Marketing Association, to remove their names from all mailing lists, which could jeopardize the efficacy of unsolicited direct mail. In their media consumption, Alphas prefer print where they can choose to read (or ignore) the advertising. When they watch television, Alphas favor public broadcasting or cable programming with limited commercial interruption, and they utilize their remote control devices to "zap" the commercials when watching conventional programming. Not surprisingly, Alphas enthusiastically embraced the VCR because it significantly enhanced their control. Some Alphas rent videocassettes on a regular basis; others with a collector's sensibility are creating their own libraries of videocassettes. Those with busy social schedules, and a high degree of organization, set their

PALOMA PICASSO
The style maker has created various products bearing her signature, from perfume to jewelry. Photo courtesy of Parfums Paloma Picasso.

VCRs in advance to record selected broadcasts in their absence (which enables them to "fast forward" the commercials during playback).

If a business fails to accommodate the Alpha consumer, he or she is likely, quite literally, to take the business into his or her own hands. For example, when faced with the high incidence of lost luggage on many airlines and the often interminable wait for their luggage if it does arrive on the plane with them, many Alpha travelers are increasingly sending their clothing ahead to their hotel destination via overnight Federal Express; a call ahead to the concierge, and their wardrobe is already unpacked when they arrive in their hotel room.

The desire for control is also reflected in Alphas' perception of freedom of choice. Even if the purchase decision has been made in advance, the Alpha consumer appreciates a selection of merchandise or service options; this consumer does not like to think that her or his freedom of choice has been limited by the proprietor or manufacturer or retailer. Restaurateurs, for example, should be prepared to accommodate the Alpha customer's culinary specifications regardless of the formal menu or standard procedure in the kitchen. Businesses offering "package deals" whether in the travel, financial services, or communications industries should provide these consumers with some flexibility or sufficient options, so that they do not feel compromised in any way. And, finally, the general Alpha disdain for many of the more obvious promotional techniques, from sweepstakes to premiums, is in one sense an extension of the desire for control: This consumer does not want to feel that a purchase decision is being manipulated by something totally extraneous to the product or service in question.

On the other hand, businesses that enhance the Alpha consumer's sense of control will profit. This may involve new products; microwave ovens, compact disk players, and telephone answering machines are recent examples. Or it may represent new ways of conducting business; for example, automatic bank tellers, toll-free customer service numbers, and convenience stores that are open 24 hours a day have enabled Alpha consumers to handle transactions whenever they want. And the growth in home delivery is leading to a renewed appreciation of services that can be performed in the home, such as haircutting and aromatherapy massage.

BRAND LOYALTY

When businesses are responsive to the values of the Alpha consumer the result is brand loyalty, the kind of brand loyalty that will enable the business to maintain a desirable image among the mainstream consumers who take their purchase cues from the Alphas. To a certain extent, the nature of Alpha brand loyalty varies by product category; for example, loyalty is particularly strong where flavor or taste is involved as in food, beverage, and tobacco, or in services, such as hair salons, restaurants, or financial institutions, where the consumer does not have the same quality control assurance present in industries that have standardized production (such as automobiles, electronics, and packaged goods). We have already addressed the key marketing elements in Alpha brand loyalty, notably the perception of quality, a clearly defined and consistent product identity, mystique, esteem, and ease of purchase. But equally important is a fundamental Alpha priority: The Alpha consumer yearns for new experiences, not new products per se. When a product performs satisfactorily, this consumer would rather repurchase it than explore the alternatives, concentrating his or her time and energy instead on the pursuit of new experiences.

TRIAL

Alpha trial purchase is generated in various ways. The identification of a new "need" (which can be anything from eyeglasses to daycare to portfolio management) is the most obvious motivation. But creating the perception of a new need often requires a subtle marketing approach; for example, a public relations program that produces favorable editorial coverage and generates positive word-of-mouth may be more persuasive than advertising. Dissatisfaction with the current product or service in question will also motivate the Alpha consumer to seek alternatives; we have already seen how deliberate this consumer can be in pursuit of product satisfaction. The introduction of a new product that represents a genuine innovation or improvement over the existing one in use will also stimulate trial; informative advertising, a focused public relations program, direct mail, or some type of "breakthrough" promotion can effectively build Alpha awareness of new products or product improvements.

New distribution may also be a factor in generating trial by Alphas. This is often the case with imported products (like cappuccino machines, Corona beer, or Vivian Westwood fashions) that the Alpha consumer had first seen on his or her foreign travels; products that had previously been available only in certain parts of the country, like Coors beer, Thomas English muffins, or Hard Rock Cafes; or products that had been available only in certain stores, like the Giorgio fragrance for women, which was initially sold exclusively at the Giorgio boutique in Beverly Hills and at Bloomingdale's. Again, advertising, public relations, direct mail, and promotion can alert the Alpha consumer.

The introduction of services that facilitate purchase, such as phone-order and home delivery, can also encourage trial. For example, the introduction of "drive-in shopping" at the innovative Vons supermarket chain in California (customers place their order for up to 10 items over a microphone at the beginning of the drive-thru and pick up their merchandise from the window at the other end three minutes later) was enthusiastically embraced by Alpha consumers.

Due to their deliberate approach to shopping and informational requirements, Alpha consumers are probably less likely than their mainstream counterparts to exhibit impulse purchase behavior. However Alphas' appreciation of visual excitement makes them very receptive to stylish design, packaging, and merchandising display; trial purchase may sometimes be the result of visual appeal, particularly for relatively low-ticket items, such as health and beauty aids or stationery, or products that are image-driven, not performance-driven, such as apparel or home furnishings.

We have attempted to provide a general understanding of

Alpha purchase behavior. In planning your targeted Alpha marketing plan, you clearly will have to analyze this consumer's purchase motivation in your industry and develop your strategy accordingly.

CHAPTER 4

MONITORING THE TRENDSETTERS

No marketer can afford to lose touch with the trendsetters, or Alpha consumers. Even if these consumers are not your regular customers, and may never be your regular customers, you must be able to anticipate their influence on your customer franchise and plan your marketing strategy accordingly. For example, Alphas are not likely to patronize fast-food restaurant chains; these restaurants simply do not correspond to their values. However, Alphas have had an enormous impact on the fast-food restaurant business in the last decade: The Alpha involvement with nutrition (including fat, cholesterol, and artificial ingredients), foreign cuisines (like Mexican, Italian, and Thai), and environmentally responsible packaging has gradually influenced many of the consumers who *do* patronize these restaurants, prompting these chains to modify their menus, culinary techniques, and packaging, or risk losing part of their existing customer base.

Monitoring the Alphas is relatively easy; it simply requires the use of your antennae to pick up the signals. The challenge for marketers and advertisers lies in the synthesis and interpretation of these signals, separating a *fad*, which presents limited opportunities for business development, from a *trend*, which has long-term implications. Jon Pareles, the perceptive pop music critic for the *New York Times* describes his methodology in a useful way: "Pop culture is so big . . . but everything is tied together . . . you just have to connect the dots."

A trend will show up simultaneously in many different places and categories; a fad is likely to be confined to a particular industry. The success of the Trivial Pursuit game, for example, was a phenomenon of the 1980s that appealed initially to Alpha consumers, (see chapter 7, Short-Term Successes) but like most fads, it did not represent any long-term marketing implications (and quickly died). On the other hand, the development of the bottled water business in this country—a $2.7-billion category[1] that was pioneered by Alpha consumers—reflected a growing awareness of holistic health, a concern with artificial ingredients, an increasing aversion to alcohol, and an involvement with environmental protection, social developments with widespread ramifications for many different industries. In other words, a trend.

The accurate identification of a trend requires an understanding of the mechanism of society. Therefore, it is imperative that marketers and advertisers look beyond their industry or product category; no business exists in a vacuum. Too many marketing professionals only monitor their direct competitors, which leads to very myopic strategic planning. (And some companies do not even recognize their real competitors: According to Laurel Cutler, vice chairman and worldwide director of marketing planning at FCB/Leber Katz Partners, New York, who served as vice president of consumer planning from 1988 to 1990 at Chrysler Corporation, the American automotive industry is "so insular, they only look at each other. It is true, you know, that the Ford reception room has three stock tickers on the desk, and they are Ford, Chrysler, and General Motors. And you wonder what is wrong with Detroit. I mean, Toyota is what should be on that desk!" With that type of tunnel vision, the decline of the American automotive industry is understandable.)[2]

Since Alphas are invariably involved at the inception of a trend, marketers should first identify Alphas, including personal acquaintances and friends, high-profile figures whose lives are chronicled in the media, and professionals in various fields whose work is usually directional—and closely monitor these people. A proven track record should be the ultimate criterion in Alpha identification because it will help you separate the trendsetters from the merely trendy. Alphas are consistently one step ahead; the merely trendy frequently falter in their attempts to keep up. *Women's Wear Daily's* "fashion victims" are a classic example.

For example, everyone knows some Alpha consumers, people

who are invariably the first among their friends to do it, buy it, wear it. Monitoring their activities, entertainment preferences, and purchase behavior in diverse categories can often be the easiest (and most entertaining) form of consumer research. Following high-profile Alphas whose lives are extensively covered in the media can also be instructive. We will briefly look at three very different "public" Alphas—Tom Wolfe, Jane Fonda, and Madonna—and examine their prophetic track records.

Novelist and journalist Tom Wolfe is perhaps the most astute social chronicler of our times. In the tradition of the great 19th-century novelists, like Thackeray and Dickens, Wolfe's works ranging from *Radical Chic* in the 1960s to *Bonfire of the Vanities* in the 1980s have succinctly defined their decades *before* they were over. Wolfe has a unique ability to crystallize the essence of a trend. For example, during the height of the "money fever" in the mid-1980s, he aptly illustrated the pervasiveness of this trend, from the Forbes 400 Wealthiest Individuals to the lowest socioeconomic level, by analyzing the symbolic importance of Mercedes-Benz as a metaphor for the decade. From investment bankers to drug dealers to the young urban blacks who stole the hood ornaments to wear around their necks as medallions, Mercedes was the car of choice. So when Mr. Wolfe announces in 1991 that a "moral fever" is replacing the "money fever," that "we are entering the granola period" and should expect to see a boom in Timberland shoes, fancy farm houses featured in *Architectural Digest*, and drug dealers trading in their Mercedes for Jeep Cherokees, marketers and advertisers should probably heed his predictions.[3]

Tom Wolfe is a highly analytical or intellectual Alpha; Jane Fonda and Madonna are more intuitive, instinctively sensing any shifts in the direction of the wind. Miss Fonda's track record is quite astonishing. For the past three decades, she has been a virtual barometer of social trends. In the early 1960s, she was at the forefront of the "sexual revolution" with her "open marriage" to the French film director, Roger Vadim, and her sex kitten film roles culminating in *Barbarella*. In the late 1960s, she became a political activist and acquired a suitably radical husband, Tom Hayden. (Miss Fonda's choice of consorts is frequently symbolic.) She has consistently espoused causes *before* they were popular, from opposition to the war in Vietnam to animal rights (she was one of the first women to decline an offer to appear in the Blackglama mink "What Becomes a Legend Most" campaign). Today, of course, Hollywood has become politically correct, and every star has to have a "cause" (and some of the more inflated egos even have to have their own "foundation"). In the 1970s during the women's movement, when women were often defined by their professional achievements, Miss Fonda concentrated on her acting career and won two Academy Awards, the ultimate validation for a film actress. In the early 1980s, she pioneered the aerobic exercise trend with her amazingly successful instructional videotapes, books, and clothing line—and earned a fortune. So when we find her in the early 1990s having breast implants, dating Ted Turner, and fly-fishing in Montana, marketers should take note.

Although Madonna has been in the spotlight for a shorter period of time, her vision is equally impressive. She was the first performer to fully exploit the potential of the music video format developed by the cable-television music network MTV, which debuted in 1981, changing the way consumers perceive pop music, television, and advertising. The whirlwind metamorphosis of the image that Miss Ciccone has presented in her videos—from Boy Toy to gamine to Material Girl to sex goddess in the tradition of Marilyn Monroe to bisexual lover—has reflected the growing celebration in our society of women's power to control their own destinies by using their feminine mystique instead of attempting to compete with men (much to the delight of Camille Paglia, the controversial sexual philosopher, and the consternation of ardent feminists). The influence of her videos in shaping trends in female imagery, fashion, and advertising in the last 8 years has been unmistakable. For example, her use of lingerie—one of the ultimate symbols of femininity—as outerwear has inspired fashion designers as diverse as Karl Lagerfeld ("I do whatever is the feeling of the moment . . . Madonna is right for the moment")[4] and Jean Paul Gaultier ("Madonna is truly incredible. She is a real American hero")[5] and has helped make the $8-billion lingerie industry the fastest growing category in women's apparel,[6] despite a sluggish retail climate. And she always engages talented directors, like David "Vogue" Fincher and Jean-Baptiste "Justify My Love" Mondino, who create very stylish videos that are clearly studied by many art directors and commercial producers. Miss Ciccone's "private" life is equally directional, whether it involves her social causes (e.g., the American Foundation for AIDS research), her taste in art (e.g., the Mexican painter, Frida Kahlo, who is just emerging from the shadow of her famous husband, Diego Rivera), or her interest in aromatherapy (e.g., the inside sleeve of her *Like a Prayer* album was scented with patchouli, an essence known for its erotic properties).

Monitoring the work of other professional marketers with proven track records is also instructive. It is important to include people from various industries because a trend may first appear outside of your immediate category or industry. We will briefly look at three visionary marketers: Ian Schrager, Patricia Field, and Neil Kraft. All three possess a fundamental understanding of hip consumers, an ability to distinguish a trend from a fad, and an unerring sense of timing, which has enabled them to develop highly successful businesses.

For the past 15 years, Ian Schrager has been on the cutting edge of contemporary tastes and values. He professes to have no marketing formula: "What I like turns out to be what everybody else likes. If I ever lose that, I'm out of business."[7] However, each of his trendsetting ventures in the high-risk nightclub and hotel businesses in New York exhibit common success factors: a fanatical attention to detail; an emphasis on design and visual excitement; a sense of theater (Mr. Schrager describes himself as "an entertainer who doesn't entertain");[8] and a cosmopolitan clientele (he likes to see "a mix ... jeans dancing with ball-gowns").[9] In the late 1970s and early 1980s when clubs were the epicenter of nightlife in New York, Mr. Schrager and his partner, the late Steve Rubell, operated two wildly successful clubs, Studio 54 and the Palladium. In the mid-1980s, when the cocaine dust started to settle on the club scene in New York, Mr. Schrager turned his attention to hotels, recognizing that hotels with their unique mix of public and private spaces might once again provide a social nucleus: He has subsequently opened the three hippest hotels in Manhattan—Morgans, The Royalton, and The Paramount. Mr. Schrager knows that Alpha consumers are not necessarily wealthy, so he has shrewdly positioned each hotel in a different price category, ranging from affordable to deluxe. However, each hotel presents a decidedly hip ambience—what Mr. Schrager calls, "a vibration, a confidence, an air."[10]

A high degree of visual excitement has characterized each of Mr. Schrager's ventures, leading *Vanity Fair* to name him "the style baron of the nineties."[11] Indeed, Mr. Schrager has consistently hired the best of the avant-garde—architects and designers like Arata Isozaki, Andree Putnam, and Philippe Starck, and artists like Kenny Scharf and Keith Haring—most of whom were unknown at the time to the general public but were respected by the Alpha consumer. Mr. Schrager has now engaged Jacques Grange to design his newest venture, the conversion of the Barbizon Hotel in Manhattan into an urban spa (scheduled to open in 1992). Marketers who ignore this new direction from Mr. Schrager do so at their own peril.

Patricia Fields is the owner of the clothing boutique in Greenwich Village bearing her name. Over the years the highly directional merchandise in Miss Field's shop has earned her the reputation as the doyenne of downtown fashion. George Wayne, who covers the club scene for *Paper* magazine, calls her "The Queen Mother of Downtown,"[12] while the *New York Times* maintains that her boutique "doubles as a daytime club for many of the city's most flamboyant night crawlers."[13] Whether they acknowledge it or not, many American fashion designers, editors, and retail buyers look to Miss Fields for direction: If they find it in her shop, it is likely to represent the beginning of a trend. For example, in the spring of 1990, Patricia Fields was featuring inexpensive acrylic wigs in 1960s-style flips and bobs; later in the year, wig-clad models started appearing in fashion magazine editorial spreads; a year later, department stores like Macy's were opening wig boutiques.

Miss Fields's merchandise often reflects her involvement with the "fashion underground." For example, Miss Fields was one of the first to recognize the potential of "vogueing," the highly stylized dance inspired by the fashion models' poses in

PATRICIA FIELD BOUTIQUE IN NEW YORK
In the playful windows styled by Jo-Jo Americo, expect the unexpected.
Here, a vinyl bustier, a bottle of Evian water, and *The Wall Street
Journal* somehow make perfect sense.

vintage issues of *Vogue* magazine. In the late 1980s when vogueing was still the exclusive domain of black drag queens in Harlem,
Miss Fields started sponsoring "House of Fields" vogueing ex-
travaganzas, which represented one of the first steps in the mainstream crossover of vogueing. Later, of course, everyone from
Madonna to the little girls on the popular ABC sitcom "Full
House" would be seen vogueing, and Jennie Livingstone would
make an award-winning documentary film, *Paris is Burning*,
about the scene in Harlem.

The innovative advertising that Neil Kraft created for Barneys New York in the 1980s played a major role in the extraor-
dinary success of the Manhattan-based specialty clothing store
(and strongly influenced the advertising of many other companies.) When Mr. Kraft became the director of Barneys' in-house
advertising department in 1984, the store did not have a distinctive advertising voice; in the next 7 years, Mr. Kraft's stylish

work established an avant-garde image for the store that helped to make it one of the few retailing success stories in the late 1980s (see chapter 7, Repositioning Success Stories).

Mr. Kraft is a former photography student with a keen understanding of visual appeal; his work consistently commands attention, including the attention of other advertising professionals. ("Everybody copies him," admits Bill Hamilton, an executive vice president at Ogilvy & Mather.[14]) In 1985, for example, Mr. Kraft hired Paula Greif, then unknown, to direct a television commercial featuring a new model, Paulina Porizkova. Shot in grainy black-and-white with rapid camera movement and a rock music soundtrack, the commercial inspired dozens of imitations. (Paula Greif was subsequently engaged by Weiden & Kennedy to direct their controversial video-verite commercial for Nike that featured the master recording of the Beatles' "Revolution," while Miss Porizkova went on to become the multi-million-dollar Estée Lauder signature model.) Similarly, a "Winter Sale" commercial in which the camera panned an empty frozen landscape was clearly a prototype for the ads later created for Infiniti cars by Hill, Holliday, Connors, Cosmopulos. Perhaps Mr. Kraft's most "influential" work for Barneys were the series of print ads shot by Annie Leibovitz featuring Barneys customers, including people of achievement who would be recognized by the Alpha consumer but not necessarily by the general public— people like Joseph Papp of the New York Shakespeare Festival and Kirk Varnedoe of the Museum of Modern Art. This approach was copied by many other advertisers, including American Express (who also hired Annie Leibovitz to take the photographs), The Gap, Hanes hosiery, and Timex watches. Mr. Kraft left Barneys in 1991 to become the image director for Esprit, the San Francisco-based clothing company; marketers and advertisers should plan to follow his career closely.

The media can be an invaluable guide in monitoring the Alpha consumers. Magazines and newspapers are essential; due to its mass market audience orientation, television is less useful. However, there is television programming, frequently on cable, that can be instructive, for example, Style With Elsa Klensch on CNN. Marketers should try to read a variety of publications

ELSA KLENSCH
The hostess of "Style with Elsa Klensch" on CNN, a fashion oriented
program with an Alpha audience.

on a regular basis, including trade press as well as the consumer press that the Alpha consumer is likely to read. Trade publications should not be limited to one's immediate industry because the emergence of a trend may first appear elsewhere, providing marketers with an opportunity to preempt their competitors. For example, you may find that *Billboard, Restaurant News, Advertising Age*, and *Women's Wear Daily* are complementary reading. The trade press will also help you monitor the diffusion of a trend in the marketplace, so that you may more accurately plan your business projections. Sometimes a trend may pass relatively quickly from the Alpha consumer to the mainstream; this is often the case with image-driven products, such as fashion or entertainment. Other times it will take years; this is usually the case with products that represent a fundamental shift in values or life-style, such as food or products with an environmentally-responsible positioning.

In a similar way, marketers should read a variety of consumer publications read by Alphas. Editorial direction, not circulation, should be the ultimate criteria in media selection because Alpha consumers are as likely to read esoteric publications, like *Paper* or the *Utne Reader*, as broader-based magazines. (See chapter 19 on Advertising for more on the Alpha media habits.) Required reading should include selected foreign magazines, notably British, French, Italian, and Japanese; even if one cannot read the editorial, the photographs and graphic design can be directional. British magazines, like *i-D* and *The Face* are particularly important (and present few comprehension barriers aside from the British sense of humor). If one had read *The Face* in the 1980s, for example, one would have been alerted to various Alpha phenomena at their inception; we will look at a few examples of prophetic editorial coverage in *The Face* and subsequent manifestations in the marketplace:

- *The introduction of* i-D *magazine (October 1980)*: The distinctive graphic style of *i-D* had a major impact on print advertising in the late 1980s, clearly influencing everyone from Nike to Bloomingdale's, and provided a visual prototype for the revamped *Details* magazine in 1990.
- *The New Psychedelia (June 1981)*: The resurgence of the 1960s in popular entertainment and fashion is just peaking 10 years later as The Doors, The Grateful Dead, Courreges, and miniskirts once again occupy center stage.
- *Tattoos (September 1981)*: Later, everyone from Johnny Depp (the young star of *Cry Baby* and *Edward Scissorhands*) to top female fashion models would sport tattoos, which became a semiotic in hip advertising, featured in ads like Guess jeans (1988) and Emporio Armani (1990).
- *Keith Haring (October 1982)*: The late graffiti-style artist was commissioned by Ian Schrager to decorate the Palladium nightclub in New York (1985), by Swatch watch to create a "limited edition" collection (1985), by Absolut vodka to create its memorable "Absolut Haring" print ad (1987), and by Chateau Mouton-Rothschild to design its label (1988), all of which appealed to Alpha consumers.
- *Hip-Hop (January 1983)*: The British term for rap music that has successfully crossed over into the mainstream, dominating the music charts and Grammy Awards in 1991 and presenting new creative opportunities for television advertising, as in the Pepsi commercials featuring MC

PAPER MAGAZINE
The downtown scene in New York. Reprinted courtesy of *Paper* magazine.

Hammer (1990) or the Taco Bell spots with Young MC (1990).

- *The American Diner (June 1983)*: The growing nostalgia for the simple, unpretentious fare and ambience of the traditional American diner has influenced restaurateurs ranging from the upscale Fog City Diner in San Francisco to Ed Debevic's (a retro diner-bar that has become a $100-million-a-year international empire with restaurants in Chicago, Phoenix, Los Angeles, New York, and Osaka, Japan) to McDonald's, which is test-marketing a new diner concept; and the image of the diner has been featured in advertising for everything from ketchup to Perry Ellis furs.

- *Bruce Weber (April 1984)*: The American photographer now creates all of the print advertising for some of the leading image makers of our time, including Ralph Lauren, Calvin Klein, and the Morgan Hotel Group. His work has been widely imitated and has even inspired nicknames, such as Weber Beach in the hip South Beach section of Miami, where Mr. Weber shot the Calvin Klein Obsession ads.

- *Philippe Starck (June 1985)*: The avant-garde French interior designer has subsequently put his highly recognizable imprimatur on everything from The Royalton hotel in New York (1988) to the packaging for Glaciér, a bottled water from Canada (1990).

- *Doc Martens Shoes (April 1986)*: The traditional British postman's shoe became a symbol of reverse-chic in the late 1980s, embraced by everyone from college students and East Village Punks to Cher and Madonna, eventually achieving mainstream exposure in *US* magazine (November 1990).

- *The Seventies Revival (February 1988)*: Although the mainstream is just now rediscovering the 1960s, the Alphas have moved on to the 1970s, which can already be seen in popular culture (e.g., the cult status of "The Brady Bunch" re-runs, Deee-lite, the return of the Eagles) and fashion (e.g., the 1991 collections of Gianni Versaci, Betsy John-

GLACIER BOTTLED WATER
The distinctive bottle, at once futuristic and reminiscent of the Ice Age, bears the unmistakable imprimatur of avant-garde French designer, Philippe Starck.

son, Yohji Yamamoto, Norma Kamali, and DKNY, complete with bell-bottoms, hot pants, and macrame sweaters).

The benediction of a hip authority like *The Face* always helps to identify Alpha trends. However, marketers should still search for additional cues or substantiation before planning their marketing strategy, because some Alpha trends may represent limited opportunities for business development. Let us look at a current example: During the period that we were writing this book, Miami—notably the South Beach area—was prominently featured in a broad range of publications covering such seemingly disparate topics as:

- *Life-style*
  Spencer Reiss in *Newsweek*, March 4, 1991: "For the young and trendy, Miami Beach is hot ... Soho by the Sea."

- *Travel*
  Mary Russell in *Spin*, November 1990: "The hottest spot in America. Here's where models, photographers, Euros and South Americans flock. New Yorkers fly down for weekends."

- *Hotels*
  Fred A. Berstein in *Metropolitan Home*, March 1991: "The Raleigh and Netherland hotels cater to hip but particular clients—people who might stay at The Royalton in New York or LA's Chateau Marmont, but not a Holiday Inn."

- *Nightlife*
  Stephen Saban in *Details*, February 1991: "A scene all shiny and new ... Miami puts New York to shame."

- *Restaurants*
  W, January 7, 1991: "News Cafe on Ocean Drive in South Beach is Miami's newest hot spot."

- *Food*
  Barbara Kafka in the *New York Times*, January 27, 1991: "Miami—the latest hotbed of American cooking."

- *Photography*
  Holly Brubach in *The New Yorker*, March 4, 1991: "Photographers and art directors began to discover that Miami has perfect light 300 days a year. New York modeling agencies like Zoli, Click, Ford and Wilhelmina opened branch offices there."
- *Fashion*
  Vogue, March 1991: The editorial was photographed on location in Miami's South Beach Art Deco district.
- *Architecture*
  Vincent Scully in *The New York Times*, January 27, 1991: "Andres Duany and Elizabeth Plater-Zyberk are by far the most interesting young architects practicing today . . . Miami plays a central role."
- *Advertising*
  Advertising Age, February 4, 1991: "A force to be reckoned with . . . hot campaigns fly at you from many directions."

This focus on Miami may turn out to be a fad with limited implications for marketers and advertisers, but it clearly merits further investigation. Signals from authorities as unrelated as Stephen Saban, an eminence grise of the club scene, and Vincent Scully, Sterling Professor of the History of Art at Yale University, suggest that marketers should presently monitor Miami in the same way they monitor New York and Los Angeles; Miami may become an important "scene" in the 1990s, as London was in the early 1960s during the Carnaby Street period or San Francisco was in the late 1960s during the Love Generation era, rich in marketing opportunities, from new products to advertising directions.

PART II

CASE STUDIES

In Part 2, we examine a broad array of products and services that appealed to the trendsetting, or Alpha, consumer in the United States in the last decade. In each case, we attempt to isolate the critical success factors, but a comprehensive analysis of each business involved is beyond the scope of this discussion. Sometimes the endorsement of the Alpha consumer was the result of skillful target marketing, for example, Absolut vodka; other times, it was largely unintentional, for example, Harley-Davidson. In some cases, the Alpha consumer is still using the product today, for example, Levi 501s; in other cases, he or she has moved on, for example, Perrier. But each case is instructive with implications for marketers and advertisers today.

The chapters have been organized according to several general scenarios that emerged:

Chapter 5: Long-Term Successes
Levi 501 jeans, Harley-Davidson, American Express, Sony

Chapter 6: Evolutionary Successes
Perrier, Club Med, MTV, *Elle* magazine

Chapter 7: Repositioning Successes
Chanel, Absolut vodka, The Gap, Barneys New York

Chapter 8:   Reverse-Chic Successes
             Marlboro cigarettes, Budweiser beer, Aqua Net
             hairspray, Kellogg's Corn Flakes
Chapter 9:   Too-Soon-To-Tell Successes
             Nike, Ben & Jerry's, Mazda Miata, The Body Shop
Chapter 10: Short-Term Successes
             Corona beer, Swatch watch, *Spy* magazine, Trivial
             Pursuit
Chapter 11: Missed Opportunities
             Avon Products, Stephen Sprouse, Tenax, Izod La-
             coste

At the end of each chapter, we attempt to identify lessons learned and discuss some of the implications and opportunities for marketers and advertisers today. As with the other sections of this book, you will have to interpret our findings within the context of your industry.

CHAPTER 5

LONG-TERM SUCCESSES

All of the following products have managed to maintain their cachet with the Alpha consumer, which has contributed to their popularity among the mainstream and their leadership positions in their categories. We will explore why certain brands can sustain their appeal for decades while other, similar products have radically shorter life cycles.

LEVI 501 JEANS

Invented by a California merchant in 1850 for use by Gold Rush miners, Levi is the original jean and an American icon. Over the years, the design and construction of the Levi 501 button-down jean has changed very little, making it closer to a commodity than a fashion product (which is usually characterized by a strategy of forced obsolescence). With their characteristic aversion to fads, Alpha consumers resisted the premium-priced designer jeans introduced by new companies in the late 1970s and early 1980s. (The designer jeans with their emphasis on new styles and fabric finishes [e.g., stone-washed] appealed to the mainstream consumer who automatically assumes that novelty or higher price-points confer status.) The Alpha consumer has remained loyal to 501s, enabling Levi Strauss & Company (1990 worldwide sales: $4.2 billion) to retain its leadership position with 21.9 percent share of the U.S. $6.6-billion jeans market.[1] The success factors in the enduring appeal of Levi jeans include:

Heritage. Levis are considered "authentic," virtually synonymous with denim pants. For the Alpha consumer with an appreciation of history and popular culture, they also carry a wealth of associations—from Gold Rush miners and cowboys to celluloid heroes like James Dean and Marlon Brando on his motorcycle. This distinctive brand identity—uniquely American, masculine, independent—was effectively reinforced in 1983 when Levi introduced its memorable "501 Blues" advertising campaign, created by its longtime agency, Foote, Cone & Belding in San Francisco. One of the first video-verite campaigns (i.e., handheld camera; grainy, documentary look; natural-looking actors including a representative ethnic mix; great, unexpected music soundtrack), it successfully depicted Levi jeans as both a uniform of the hip and an individual fashion statement.

Integrity. Alphas respect the fact that product styling does not change according to the vagaries of fashion. (It is interesting to note that, with the exception of the Dockers line of casual clothes, which represents sales of about $600 million,[2] the company's ventures into other apparel categories have not been successful. Robert Haas, the company's CEO has conceded, "When we start veering into fashion, we have problems."[3]) Alphas also like the fact that Levis are so well-constructed that they last for years and actually improve with age, acquiring that faded patina which identifies the wearer as a survivor. Moreover, Alpha consumers have the self-confidence to buy new jeans and "break them in" personally (while some mainstream consumers purchase "prewashed" jeans and others pay outrageous prices for vintage Levis at trendy stores like Mark Fox in Los Angeles where Kevin Costner, Tom Cruise, and Julia Roberts shop).[4]

Versatility. Alphas appreciate the timeless versatility of the Levi jean, which can be worn by virtually anyone in whatever manner he or she chooses. There are no sartorial rules or socio economic distinctions where Levis are concerned; Levis are worn by the construction worker on the job, the punk rocker, and Ralph Lauren in his tuxedo jacket. It should be noted that Levi's decidedly masculine brand identity has weakened its appeal for some women. (In the women's market, Lee is the leading brand.) Nevertheless, Levi jeans have been worn by many prominent women, as diverse as Marilyn Monroe and Annette de la Renta (the wife of the fashion designer and heiress apparent to Brooke Astor in New York's social firmament).

HARLEY-DAVIDSON

Like Levi 501 jeans, Harley-Davidson motorcycles are American icons with a rich heritage in popular culture. (Even though Marlon Brando, in his black leather jacket and Levi jeans, did not actually ride a Harley in *The Wild One*, everyone thinks he did.) The success of Harley-Davidson is the result of its ability to maintain its tough, rebellious brand identity while broadening its appeal beyond hard-core bikers. As Kathleen Demitros, the vice president of marketing, noted, "We had to find a way to balance our image more, without turning it into 'white bread' and making it bland."[5] Harley-Davidson represents one of the most interesting business turn-around stories of the 1980s. The unreliable quality of the products was jeopardizing Alpha brand loyalty, while mainstream consumers were increasingly buying lower-priced Japanese imports. In 1983 the company was on the verge of bankruptcy. But even the U.S. Congress harbored a secret nostalgia for Harley-Davidson, the only remaining American manufacturer of motorcycles, and they imposed a stiff 49 percent tariff on Japanese imports from 1983 to 1986, providing the company with time to regain its competitive edge. Harley-Davidson accomplished this by focusing on its heritage, notably the big bikes affectionately known throughout the world as "Hogs" with their high price-points (e.g., $15,000) and handsome margins; improving product quality; and recognizing that many affluent professionals—from the late Malcolm Forbes to Hollywood Brat Packers—longed to fulfill their fantasies as weekend rebels. The company increased its share of the market for big bikes from 23 percent in 1983 to 60 percent in 1989 and saw its net income surge to a record $32.9 million on sales of $791 million.[6] The Harley-Davidson success factors include:

Mystique. As Vaughn Beals, the Harley-Davidson chairman, has noted, Harley-Davidson "is the only product name I've ever seen that people tattoo on their bodies."[7] That kind of fanatical brand loyalty has contributed significantly to the product's mystique. It is partly the result of the company's heritage, partly the result of its dedication to its hard-core customers (the Hells Angels set), and partly the result of product design that is in many ways antidesigner in its orientation (much like the Levi 501 jean). As William Davidson, grandson of a founder, now a co-owner and the company's styling vice president, explains, "They really know what they want on their bikes . . . It has to do something for your ego."[8] Consequently, the Harley-Davidson bikes celebrate their hardware in direct contrast to the sleek new Japanese models, which conceal it, and styling changes are subtle; a new Harley is not radically different in appearance from a vintage model.

Management.   Most of the Harley-Davidson management team are bikers. Some, like Mr. Davidson, are lifelong aficionados; others, like Mr. Beals, were newcomers ("Like many of the people who have got into biking as professional managers, I became a dyed-in-the-wool enthusiast").[9] But they all share a passion for biking that enables them to stay in touch with their customers. According to Mr. Beals, "Our relationship with cyclists is one of the differences between us and our Japanese competitors."[10]

AMERICAN EXPRESS

Although credit cards went from status symbols to commodities available to almost anyone in the 1980s, American Express has managed to maintain its cachet among Alpha consumers by providing excellent service, emphasizing its heritage in travel and entertainment, and positioning the product as an exclusive luxury good ("Membership has its privileges"). Despite the fact that the credit card business has become a parity market with little differentiation in product benefits, American Express enjoys a certain consumer esteem that Visa and MasterCard lack. This is due in part to the company's total control of its business; the quality of the service provided by Visa and MasterCard depends on the bank that issues the card, and there is limited quality

AMERICAN EXPRESS PRINT AD
The memorable campaign photographed by Annie Leibovitz presented
historically documented "users" in unexpected situations which made
the celebrities featured appear particularly appealing and accessible.
Here, the unlikely pairing of Wilt Chamberlain and Willie Shoemaker.
Reprinted with permission of American Express Travel Related Services
Co., Inc.

Wilt Chamberlain. Cardmember since 1976.
Willie Shoemaker. Cardmember since 1966.

*Membership
Has Its Privileges.*

Don't leave home without it.
Call 1-800-THE CARD to apply.

control. American Express is able to control its image more completely. "These days the best product doesn't win anymore," says Joanne Black, a former AmEx and MasterCard marketing executive, now president of Black & Associates. "When you use a card, you have to feel about it like you feel about a person."[11] Alpha users feel good about American Express; AmEx's charge volume in 1989 increased 11 percent to $65 billion. (It should be noted, however, that the AmEx share of the credit card market declined in 1989 from 22.6 percent to 21.9 percent as Visa continues to make inroads among mainstream consumers who are somewhat intimidated by American Express—both its ultraexclusive image and its full-payment requirement each month.[12]) The critical success factors in the enduring Alpha esteem of American Express include:

Heritage and a distinctive brand identity. From its introduction in 1958, the American Express card has been marketed as a luxury good. It was primarily for use with airlines, hotels, and restaurants around the world at a time when foreign travel was less common. Ownership of a universal credit card was a "privilege," and the 250,000 people who bought one did feel "special." Although 36 million people now have AmEx cards (and 190 million have Visa cards),[13] American Express has been able to maintain this esteem with a consistent positioning; an emphasis on its glamorous heritage in foreign travel (e.g., the local American Express office is often a major presence and destination point for financial transactions, travel arrangements, and communications in foreign cities) and entertainment (e.g., American Express reserves a limited number of select seats to hit Broadway shows for its Gold Card members); "persuading" some image-enhancing stores, like Neiman Marcus, to accept only the American Express cards (in exchange for agreeing not to take Visa or MasterCard, these stores have had their AmEx merchant discounts significantly reduced, and they receive valuable free advertising from American Express);[14] and last, but not least, by charging a premium price for the "privilege" of owning an AmEx card. (Annual fees on the green and gold cards are now $55 and $75—substantially higher than the competition.) When you are marketing a luxury good, competing on price is self-defeating.

(The company's recent strategy to broaden its customer base by venturing into mass market stores and fast-food restaurants is a risky one; it could diminish the distinctive identity the company has so successfully created and jeopardize Alpha brand loyalty.)

Advertising.   The membership concept with its inherent insider's appeal has been effectively reinforced in television and print advertising featuring spokespersons who are "cardmembers," one of the few cases where celebrity advertising has enhanced the brand's identity in the minds of the Alpha consumer because the spokesperson is a documented user. (Occasionally it does raise questions: Meryl Streep became a star in the late 1970s but she did not become a cardmember until 1983. . . . One wonders what she did before that.) In its "Do You Know Me" television commercials beginning in 1974 and its "Cardmember Since _____" print ads created by celebrity photographer Annie Leibovitz beginning in 1987, a fascinating array of cardmembers have been featured; for example, Broadway composer Stephen Sondheim, Boston Opera director Sarah Caldwell, fashion designer Bill Blass, pro football coach Tom Landry, former House Speaker Tip O'Neill, and Christian rock star Amy Grant. The advertising campaigns have benefited from their continuity of format: Consumers know it is an American Express ad before they identify the cardmember, so the celebrity association enhances the product instead of overshadowing it (which is often the case with celebrity endorsements). At the same time, this Hall of Fame approach has made an appearance in an American Express ad not only acceptable but also quite desirable in the eyes of the spokespersons (according to perennial best-selling author Stephen King, "It's just such a compliment. . . . Certainly it's not going to do much for my literary reputation although many would say I don't have a literary reputation to worry about").[15] And it has enabled the company to frequently engage "virgin" celebrities (including long-term holdouts like actor Paul Newman) who are not tarnished by other endorsements. Of course, the impact of the advertising has been aided by heavy media spending, for example, $124 million in 1990.

SONY

In the last 30 years the perception of the "Made in Japan" product identification has radically changed, from one of substandard quality to one of technological excellence, and Sony electronics are a major reason. The Sony Corporation of America has introduced a constant stream of innovative, superior-quality products that are always on the cutting edge of design and technology. Despite increasing competition from other lower-priced imports, Americans are willing to pay a premium for Sony quality. In 1990, Sony sold $15 billion worth of audio and video electronics in this country. The Sony success factors include:

Product innovation.   In consumer electronics, Sony has consistently set the pace with an amazing series of product innovations: the all-transistor radio, the transistorized TV, the videocassette recorder, the Trinitron color television system, the Walkman, the camcorder. This has enabled the company to consistently create a sense of new consumer needs—perhaps the ultimate challenge for the marketer—compelling people to continually upgrade their electronics. Sony management recognizes that most of its electronics products are nonessential purchases, so they have a "10 times" rule of thumb according to Yuki Nozoe, vice president of the personal-video division: Any major new Sony product is designed to offer a combination of attractions that make it 10 times better than rivals or predecessors.[16] Stylish design is a vital element, particularly where female consumers are involved; for example, the company says that white is a visual symbol of user-friendliness that appeals to women, the opposite of the high-tech professional overtones of black, and thus designs certain products accordingly. (It should be noted that women accounted for 40 percent of all videocassette recorder sales, 41% of all compact disk sales, and 58 percent of all console stereo systems sales in the United States in 1989 according to New York-based Simmons Market Research.[17])

Niche marketing.   When Sony introduces a new product, it targets sophisticated, knowledgeable consumers who are very involved with electronics and willing to pay a premium price—

in other words, the Alpha consumer—with limited distribution and highly focused advertising and public relations programs (e.g., Sony loaned camcorders to the University of Southern California's film school). When competitors catch up with lower-priced versions, Sony moves quickly to broaden its lines and segment the mass market. For example, the company sold 30,000 Walkmans when the product was introduced in the United States at a $200 retail price-point in 1979. They gradually expanded the line, both upward and downward, with technical innovations (e.g., water-resistant) and life-style models (e.g., My First Sony for kids). Today there are about 70 models, and sales are about 30,000 a day.

LESSONS LEARNED

Category pioneers like Levi Strauss, Harley-Davidson, American Express, and Sony, who are virtually synonymous with their categories, frequently enjoy a distinct competitive advantage in the minds of Alpha consumers with their keen respect for originality and authenticity. Businesses with a long-term perspective should emphasize research and innovation with the objective of developing new products and services that will enable them to pioneer new categories of business and reap the historical advantage.

Superior quality and a distinct brand identity are key to developing Alpha consumer brand loyalty. Over the years, the basic positioning of Levi Strauss, Harley-Davidson, American Express, and Sony consumer electronics have remained the same; this consistency has been reinforced by a strong visual signature (in the case of the three product manufacturers—Levi Strauss, Harley-Davidson, and Sony) and logical line extensions that have not diluted the equity in the original product.

In the case of the older companies, Levi Strauss and Harley-Davidson, and, to a somewhat lesser extent, American Express and Sony, the distinct brand identity and heritage have imbued these businesses with an undeniable mystique that translates into an invaluable, if somewhat intangible, sense of consumer esteem. Indeed, a Harley-Davidson "Hog," a pair of Levi 501 jeans, or an American Express card is almost a cult product, a clear communication symbol among consumers.

All four businesses have successfully maintained their cult status because they never lost touch with their Alpha consumers. Whether it is the Hell's Angel at Harley-Davidson, the urbane world traveler at American Express, or the audio-video-phile at Sony, each company has skillfully broadened their customer base without alienating these influential core users.

Stylish advertising that updates the brand's heritage may help it remain contemporary as we saw with the Levi "501 Blues" television commercials or the American Express "Cardmember Since _____" print campaign. But this is not essential; the impact on the Alpha consumer of the Harley-Davidson and Sony advertising was negligible.

CHAPTER 6

EVOLUTIONARY SUCCESSES

Initially targeted at Alpha consumers with a hip sensibility, the following products gradually broadened their consumer franchises over a period of 5 to 10 years. They took so long for the mainstream to adopt the brand, that they were not perceived as an overnight sensation or a fad. Although the Alpha consumer has defected, this has had a marginal impact on the brand's popularity in the eyes of the mainstream consumer who considers these products classics. We will examine the reasons for the initial endorsement—and subsequent rejection—by the Alpha consumer and explore the role played by the Alpha consumer in the creation of a desirable brand image.

PERRIER

Perrier pioneered the bottled water industry in the United States and became synonymous with the category. "Perrier was like Kleenex—it was second nature to ask for it," according to Ansell Hawkins, owner of New York's hip Odeon restaurant. "That second nature came from being the first and only choice for so long."[1] In the decade following its introduction in this country in 1976, consumption of bottled water tripled, and Perrier's U.S. sales reached $140 million (before a voluntary worldwide product recall in 1990—after traces of benzene, a suspected carcinogen, were found in some bottles—destroyed the brand's momentum).[2]

Perrier's initial success with Alpha consumers was the result of uncanny timing, a stylish and distinctive bottle, a chic "designer" positioning at a time when this approach to beverage marketing was a novelty, the Imported-From-France heritage, and distribution in image-enhancing restaurants, bars, and hotels (which represented a third of the Perrier business in this country). Furthermore, many Alphas were already familiar with Perrier from their foreign travels, which contributed to its insider's cachet when it was introduced in this country. At the same time, Perrier benefited from the growing awareness of holistic health, the concern with the artificial ingredients found in soft drinks, and the decline in liquor consumption.

However, Perrier gradually lost its mystique for the Alpha consumer when it became an aspirational status symbol in the 1980s narrowly associated with people who were drinking it for the wrong reasons—the people with Rolex watches, Filofaxes, and BMWs. The Alpha consumer did not want to risk confusion regarding purchase motivation and moved on to other brands of imported waters that were then available, like Evian and San Pellegrino. (Today more than 700 brands of bottled water are sold in this country, and restaurants that once carried only Perrier now carry several different brands.) The brand's mystique was further eroded in the late 1980s when the company started pursuing a highly visible discount strategy with coupons in newspaper supplements and "buy-two-get-one-free" promotions in supermarkets; once you assume a promotional posture, you immediately devalue your product in the eyes of the consumer.

CLUB MED

Like Perrier, Club Med benefited from its French image. When the first Club Med opened in 1950, it was a revolutionary concept in tourism: "They found out how to produce resorts at a low cost in exotic places and lure adults to what is basically a sophisticated summer camp," noted Somerset Waters, travel industry analyst.[3] Initially embraced by hedonistic Alpha consumers, which contributed to its hip image, Club Med has evolved over the years into a $1-billion business that caters to the mainstream with "family" packages, corporate programs, cruise ships, and trips organized around special instruction in everything from golf to underwater photography.

Alphas originally responded to the uniqueness of the Club Med concept—its aspect of total escape ("The Antidote to Civilization"), club "membership," unlocked doors, rooms without telephones, and all-inclusive packages that obviated the need for money and credit cards. The appeal was enhanced by beautiful locations; good and reliable cuisine; and the persistent French ambience due as much to its loyal French clientele as its French G.O.s, or Gentil Organisateurs, the attractive young people who run each "village."

But from the perspective of the Alpha consumer, Club Med was a victim of its own success: When it started attracting people who longed to join the swinging singles, wet T-shirt set, the Alpha consumer defected. As Club Med increasingly catered to the mainstream, it lost much of the unique character that had appealed initially to the Alpha consumer. Today, many Club Med villages are indistinguishable from conventional resort hotels—televisions and telephones in the rooms, locks on the doors, annex restaurants with sit-down service—and the clientele has lost its international flavor. (In the 1980s, Americans and Japanese accounted for 60 percent of Club Med's growth, English became the dominant language in many villages, and Americans now represent 25 percent of the G.O.s.[4]) Of course, this has only enhanced its appeal for the mainstream vacationer who is now the Club Med customer, and 47 percent of them return for repeat visits—one of the highest rates of recidivism in the travel industry.[5] For these relatively unadventurous travelers, Club Med provides a safe and easy opportunity to visit a foreign country with little of the uncertainty associated with independent travel and more glamour than taking an organized tour.

MTV

When MTV, the music television cable channel started broadcasting rock music video clips 24 hours a day on August 1, 1981, Alphas immediately responded to its novelty. With its hip, frequently irreverent sensibility, its modular structure, its nonlinear storytelling, MTV was everything that conventional television was not. Although Alpha viewers recognized that the music videos were promotions first and artistic statements second, the novelty of the execution—a unique hybrid of imagery and sound—initially sustained their interest. And the brevity of the form (most videos last only three to five minutes) made it easier to endure less creative ones. Alphas also responded to the 24 hours-a-day format, which enabled them to tune in whenever they felt like it; at 6:00 a.m. you might have found an early riser and a club kid who had not yet gone to bed watching the same video. MTV launched in only 1.5 million homes in 1981; the limited availability of MTV—for example, it was not available in Manhattan until September 1, 1982—contributed to its initial allure and hip, almost underground image. This was reinforced with an innovative direct response marketing campaign, "I Want MY MTV," featuring high-profile rock stars like Mick Jagger and Sting, who urged viewers to call their cable service and demand the new channel, and quirky promotions, like the John Cougar Mellencamp "Paint the Mother Pink" contest, which elicited more than 200,000 entries. (The first prize was a weekend in Bloomington, Indiana, with 25 of your closest friends, where you would meet John Cougar Mellencamp—the least pretentious of rock stars—and paint a house pink; they gave you the house.)

Today, MTV reaches 46.1 million people over 5,340 affiliates across the country,[6] but it is watched less frequently by the Alpha viewer (who tunes in primarily to see new videos). There are several reasons for the Alpha defection. When the music video format first appeared, Alphas had hoped that it would become a new art form that would attract serious artists. With a few notable exceptions, this has not happened; a typical music video still revolves around a performer who lip-syncs the song. Moreover, most new ideas are so widely imitated in other videos, commercials, movies, and television shows that they quickly become clichés. As MTV gradually attracted a mainstream audience, the station came under increasing pressure from timid advertisers to ban videos that might incite controversy, for example, Madonna's "Justify My Love" video in 1991. This double standard has severely compromised the perceived integrity of MTV and has caused it to lose its cutting edge image. Some Alpha viewers were further alienated by the increasing deviation from the original continuous music programing format (e.g., scheduled shows like the "Remote Control" game show and the "Club MTV" dance show) designed to broaden the MTV audience.

ELLE

When Hachette Publications introduced an American version of its French fashion magazine *Elle* in 1985, it was an immediate sensation among Alpha women. They were bored with the sameness of the American fashion magazines and responded to the innovations that *Elle* introduced, including the oversize look, the bold graphics, the stylish editorial spreads, and the high-gloss paper. The magazine's chic image was reinforced by its French fashion "authority"; its upscale advertisers (the publishers refused to accept advertising from mass market manufacturers whom they did not consider image-enhancing; for example, with characteristic Gallic chauvinism, L'Oréal cosmetics was deemed acceptable while Maybelline was not); and its sophisticated "*Elle* Is" advertising campaign created by Peter Rogers Associates in New York, which highlighted the magazine's distinctive graphic design (its best product feature).

Unfortunately, the quality of the editorial did not match the look of the magazine. It was one-note editorial that did not evolve, and the Alpha reader gradually lost interest. (For example, black models wearing neon-colored clothes photographed against an all-white background was visually arresting the first time, but it soon became all too formulaic.) And *Elle*'s graphic design was so widely imitated in print advertising and other fashion magazines that the magazine lost its sense of differentiation. Moreover, the Alpha reader was further alienated by the magazine's marketing programs designed to increase circulation and profitability at the expense of the product's image: Mass market advertising was accepted; the distinctive oversize format was reduced to standard magazine size; and the magazine became a major presence at newsstands and supermarket checkout counters, joining the *Enquirer, TV Guide,* and *Family Circle*; there was heavy discounting for new subscribers ("Save 59% off the newsstand cost!") and extensive merchandising of *Elle* signature premiums, like tote bags (always a high-risk proposition for businesses in image-driven industries because the chances that the user will enhance your image are slight indeed). The Alpha reader moved on: Some returned to *Vogue* when Anna Wintour became editor bringing the magazine a somewhat British slant. Some embraced *Mirabella*, the upscale new publication started by Grace Mirabella when Condé Nast unceremoniously gave her job at *Vogue* to Anna Wintour (according to the *New York Times*, in the opinion of most fashion designers, *Mirabella* is now second to *Vogue*, overtaking *Elle* in prestige).[7] Others are increasingly reading European fashion magazines, which are frequently characterized by more adventurous editorial. But this is just beginning to have an impact on the aspirational mainstream reader who associates *Elle* with high fashion: Newsstand sales have declined 17 percent in 1991. Still, *Elle* has a circulation of 837,000 with ad revenues of $68 million in 1990[8] and a new editorial staff who may successfully revitalize the book, so it would be premature to predict its demise.

LESSONS LEARNED

Novelty or innovation may attract the initial interest of the Alpha consumer, but brand loyalty is founded on the basis of a perceived differential advantage. When Perrier, Club Med, MTV, and *Elle* first appeared, each was a novelty without direct competitors at the time. However, novelty was not a sufficient foundation for brand loyalty. In the case of Perrier, competitive entries contributed to its demise. Club Med altered its original product concept and alienated its Alpha franchise. MTV and *Elle*, on the other hand, failed to alter their original product concepts and lost many of their Alpha customers once the novelty wore off.

With their predisposition to foreign products, Alpha consumers are invariably the first to adopt new imports or products with a foreign heritage; the French origins of Perrier, Club Med, and *Elle* contributed significantly to their initial appeal for Alpha consumers.

The initial endorsement of the influential Alpha consumer can create a highly desirable brand identity for a new business in the eyes of the mainstream. Perrier, Club Med, MTV, and

Elle successfully targeted Alpha consumers for market development with limited distribution strategies and an emphasis on exclusivity; when the Alpha consumer defected, few mainstream consumers noticed because they considered these products classics.

CHAPTER 7

REPOSITIONING SUCCESSES

Businesses and products with outdated or unexciting brand images can be successfully revitalized when they target the trendsetting consumer. We will look at four repositioning successes—Chanel, Absolut vodka, The Gap, and Barneys New York—and analyze the role played by the Alpha consumer. A successful repositioning cannot be too abrupt; it should be perceived as a logical business evolution. Barneys New York, for example, evolved from an unexciting, moderately priced men's clothing store into a high-fashion specialty store for men and women, but it remained an apparel retailer. This type of gradual change requires a long-term commitment that is seldom found in American corporations today with their emphasis on short-term profitability. It is probably significant that Chanel and Barneys are privately held. In most instances, it also requires a singular vision that is equally rare in corporations today with their bureaucratic decision-making procedures. Sometimes this visionary leadership is provided by the company CEO or president; this was the case with Donald Fisher at The Gap and Michel Roux at Carillon Importers, which markets Absolut vodka. Sometimes it is provided by the owner, the Pressman family at Barneys, for example. Other times, senior management needs to recruit new talent to supply the vision; this was the case when Alain Wertheimer, the chairman of Chanel, hired fashion designer Karl Lagerfeld in 1982 to make all design and image decisions for the moribund house of one of France's most revered fashion icons. This autocratic outlook usually extends to the advertising; it is no coincidence that most of the advertising for Chanel, The Gap, and Barneys is created in-house—and Mr. Roux was responsible for the introduction of contemporary artists like Andy Warhol into the Absolut vodka advertising in 1985, which represented the "breakthrough" in that campaign. (Mr. Roux wisely overruled the objections of TBWA, Inc., the New York advertising agency that handles the Absolut account: "They said, 'You're crazy—we can't do that,' but I said, 'It's Warhol—that's image'.") Finally, it should be noted that the introduction of new products frequently facilitates a repositioning. This was certainly the case at Chanel, The Gap, and Barneys. But even at Chanel, the Chanel No. 5 fragrance, introduced in 1923, remains a cornerstone of that business.

CHANEL

In the past 15 years, Chanel has evolved from a venerable, but very tired, company whose business in the United States was largely dependent on one product, the Chanel No. 5 fragrance, into one of the most important forces in fashion today with a growing empire in apparel, accessories, shoes, and cosmetics sold in about 500 prestige specialty and department stores and in its own retail stores. Today the consumer demand for anything Chanel is approaching fanaticism. Andy Basile, the fashion director of Bergdorf Goodman, recently noted, "Some women were fighting over the clothes. When we told them we were all out of certain items, they didn't believe us. One woman said, 'If I can't have those leggings, I'll die'."[1] Ira Neimark, chairman of Bergdorf Goodman, added, "Chanel is going through the roof."[2]

The Chanel success is the result of a long-term strategy to make Chanel totally contemporary yet still identifiably Chanel, attracting a new generation of hip young women without alienating the traditional Chanel customer. The decision to hire Karl Lagerfeld (dubbed "The Kaiser" by *Women's Wear Daily*) in 1982 to revitalize the Chanel image was the pivotal event in this transformation. Alain Wertheimer, the chairman of Chanel, explained his rationale in engaging the iconoclastic German-born designer: "I knew he was the one. People had tried before to revive Chanel with respect. But you can't stand still, in fashion or in business."[3] Mr. Lagerfeld did not disappoint. With wit

("Good taste is like a red light. Everything stops dead"[4]) and irreverence ("Any designer who refuses to look at the street is an idiot. That's where ideas are coming from for the last twenty years"[5]) and a keen sense of parody and inversion ("For Chanel, I have to work within the structure of the Chanel, like an actor bringing his own style to a part"[6]), Mr. Lagerfeld has totally rejuvenated Chanel. As Bernadine Morris, the fashion editor of the *New York Times*, noted, "Chanel started in the early part of the 20th century; Mr. Lagerfeld makes the clothes look ready for the 21st."[7]

Mr. Lagerfeld's accomplishment has been reinforced with highly synergistic marketing. Everything the company does enhances the distinctive image that he has created. Merchandising, marketing, and advertising programs are uniform all over the world. Premium pricing is maintained in every product category. There is little overt promotion. In apparel and accessories, for example, there is a constant flow of new merchandise and frequent sellouts; there are few markdowns—and only twice a year at the end of the fashion "season." In cosmetics and fragrances, business is built on product sampling—in stores, at image-enhancing charity events, and in targeted direct marketing programs—not on the "gift-with-purchase" and "purchase-with-purchase" strategy adopted by so many competitors, which only devalues your product in the minds of the consumer. Line extensions have been logical; the company has resisted the temptation to enter product categories that are not fashion-related. For example, the introduction of premium-priced makeup and skincare products—now a $95-million business for Chanel in the United States[8]—simultaneously upgraded the Chanel image in this country and expanded the cosmetics franchise built upon the fragrances. Distribution has been significantly reduced; today, Chanel products are only sold in better specialty and department stores where the company usually invests in distinctive Chanel boutiques—separate retailing environments that reinforce the exclusive Chanel identity—or in the company-owned Chanel stores. The company always "protects" the Chanel image. For example, they seldom participate in storewide catalogs that include other manufacturers, preferring to send their own mail pieces where they can control the image and the distribution.

It should be noted that the strength of the Chanel brand identity in women's fashion and beauty products may have hindered their development of the men's market in this country. The Chanel men's products, notably fragrances, neckties, and accessories, are generally bought by women who love "anything Chanel" as gifts for men and do not represent significant volume. "We haven't yet become a dramatic factor in the men's market," admits Arie Kopelman, president of Chanel, Inc. in the United States. "Chanel has very strong feminine connotations," agreed Laurie Palma, vice president of fragrance marketing.[9] It remains to be seen whether the introduction of the Égoïste fragrance for men in 1991 can alter this purchase pattern.

ABSOLUT VODKA

In 1979, Absolut was a tiny vodka brand selling about 12,000 cases a year; in 1990, Absolut sold 2.7 million cases and was the #1 imported vodka with 58 percent of the category.[10] The success of Absolut was due to the growth in the vodka category as Americans increasingly shifted from other distilled spirits and to the repositioning of the brand as a "designer" product in 1980 with the introduction of the unique advertising campaign featuring the distinctive Absolut bottle in a series of ads that played upon the name. Richard Lewis, senior vice president/management supervisor at TBWA in New York, the agency that handles the campaign, recalls, "We weren't just selling another vodka. We wanted to make this a fashionable product . . . like perfume."[11] Absolut became so fashionable that it succeeded in "taking drinkers away from other categories, particularly young premium drinkers," according to Frank Walters, director of research for M. Shanken Communications, publishers of alcoholic beverage industry trades *Impact* and *Market Watch*.[12]

The Alpha consumer initially responded to the novelty of the advertising—the focus on the product, the clever wordplay on the Absolut name, the total absence of the product "users" so conspicuous in most liquor advertising at the time, and its presence in many offbeat magazines. This interest has been maintained with the growing involvement of artists, fashion designers, and musicians in the Absolut marketing program, from the participation of artists like Kenny Scharf in the advertising campaign to the company's philanthropy like the "Absolut Concerto" concerts it underwrites at New York's Lincoln Center, in which new orchestral works commissioned by American composers are performed with the proceeds benefiting the Manhattan School of Music.

This highly personal involvement with the arts and fashion reflects the vision of Michel Roux, the president of Carillon Importers, which distributes Absolut. (Carillon Importers is a subsidiary of Grand Metropolitan PLC, the British conglomerate.) Mr. Roux is passionate about the arts; he is using this passion to sell vodka: "If you are able to reach people and touch them—and not always with the same thing—you will achieve your goal of creating a consumer." Mr. Roux clearly relishes his growing role as a cultural impresario: "Can you imagine if you were just a booze peddler?" As we noted, Mr. Roux was responsible for the introduction of artists into the Absolut advertising campaign in 1985, and it is his relentless pursuit of the avant-garde that has enabled the brand to retain its leading edge image. However, Mr. Roux recognizes the importance of consistency and the long-term brand equity he is building: "I tell all my people to keep everything related to Absolut because one day all the things will be collected—maybe 15 or 20 years from now, maybe sooner—but people will be selling them in antique shops." (This is already starting: Andy Warhol signed 100 of his Absolut ad posters, which are now worth $10,000.)

Mr. Roux is equally involved in the innovative Absolut media planning, which includes offbeat, untested magazines with small audiences (often with questionable purchasing power) as well as mainstream publications. Mr. Roux understands that the Alpha readers of the more esoteric magazines have been a critical factor in establishing the trendsetting brand image Absolut enjoys. The Absolut media planning is further distinguished by a high level of frequency in each publication and a sensitivity to the reader's state of mind, which often encourages Mr. Roux to tailor the creative for the audience: "You read different magazines for different reasons. When you read *Time*, you are not in the same state of mind as when you read *Interview*. A 'fashion' ad in *Time* would mean very little, but in *Vogue*. . . ."

Like Chanel, Mr. Roux recognizes the danger of discounting: "I will never discount . . . I would rather lose volume. When you reduce your price, you are telling the customer that the week before 'I robbed you.' Few people know how to preserve their image—like the fashion designers who sell to retail stores whom they know will discount their merchandise—and then they wonder why they lose their image."

THE GAP

The Gap stores were founded in 1969 by Donald G. Fisher who remains the company's CEO and guiding visionary. Then a 40-year-old realtor, Mr. Fisher had difficulty finding a pair of Levi jeans that fit him and discovered that few department stores carried in-depth stocks of Levi Strauss products: Mr. Fisher identified a business opportunity and opened a shop that specialized in Levi Strauss products.

The Gap experienced tremendous growth in the 1970s, but Mr. Fisher recognized the potential danger of dependence on denim products—and one manufacturer. He started introducing private-label merchandise, and, in the early 1980s, decided to reposition The Gap, primarily as a private-label casual sportswear company. In 1983, Mr. Fisher recruited a new company president, Millard S. (Mickey) Drexler, the president of the Ann Taylor chain of women's specialty stores, to help him execute his repositioning strategy. The Gap remains a narrow and deep classification business, but the emphasis shifted from denim to colorful and stylish casual clothes in natural fibers, which offer considerable consumer value. As designer, merchandiser, marketer, and retailer of most of its products, The Gap is one of the most vertically integrated companies in the country, which enables it to enjoy better margins while passing along significant savings to the consumer. The distinctive print advertising created by the in-house agency successfully established a new image for The Gap consistent with the repositioning. The new strategy has produced remarkable results: Annual sales increased from about $650 million in 1985 to just under $2 billion in 1990; profits increased in a 10-year period from $27,700,000 to $97,600,000;[13] annual sales-per-square-foot average $450;[14] there are now nearly 800 Gap stores and 150 GapKids stores.[15]

With his specialty store orientation and appreciation of a clear brand identity, the Alpha consumer responded favorably to The Gap repositioning. The Alpha consumer liked the narrow and deep focus of the merchandise; there was no confusion about the store's identity. Daniel. E. Walker, vice president of human resources noted, "The most predictable path to failure is to become unpredictable to the customer. She needs to know what you stand for. She has limited time and will go to another store if you confuse her. The concept of loyalty doesn't apply to retail customers."[16] Alphas also appreciated the emphasis on natural fibers, the classic styling of many products (which enabled the consumer to wear them with everything from a black leather motorcycle jacket to a designer blazer), and the value they represented. At the same time, the ubiquity of the stores in downtown and neighborhood areas (there are 29 in New York City alone), the constant flow of new merchandise (always seductively displayed in the windows), and the accessible price-points encouraged impulse purchase. Alphas also appreciated the maintenance of the stores and the consistently high level of customer service. As Mr. Walker recognized, "A shabby or out-of-date shop sends a clear message to everyone—you don't really care. At The Gap, we are always remodeling. We want our stores to look fresh and act as a clean, efficient backdrop for our merchandise."[17]

In the late 1980s, Alpha consumers also responded positively to The Gap's "Individuals of Style" print advertising campaign (which won back-to-back Clio awards). Alphas liked the stylish black-and-white photographs by celebrity photographer Herb Ritts; the eclectic group of individuals appearing in the ads, ranging from superstars like movie actress Kim Basinger to "cult" figures largely unknown outside of Alpha circles—people like Santo Loquasto, the stage and film designer, or Larry Rivers, the artist; the irreverent way the personalities wore a single item of Gap apparel, such as a basic turtleneck shirt, with their own non-Gap clothing. Despite the success of the campaign, The Gap recognized the importance of novelty in advertising—and a growing consumer backlash to the excessive celebrity advertising of the 1980s—and started phasing out the "Individuals of Style" campaign in 1990, replacing it with color photographs of up-and-coming models clothed entirely by The Gap. "You can't stay with something forever" says Mr. Drexler.[18] (Although mainstream consumers may find it easier to relate to the new print advertising, Alphas would have liked to see the company continue the "Individuals of Style" campaign; as with the American Express or Absolut vodka print campaigns, Alphas were very involved and looked forward to the next in the series.) In an effort to reach a broader audience, The Gap also returned to television advertising in 1991 after focusing for many years exclusively on the print strategy that had proven so effective in reaching the Alpha consumer. The new television campaign featured a broad range of people of various ages with the new copy platform "For every generation there's a Gap." The commercials were filmed in black and white to provide some continuity with the print campaign; this is the only reference to the "Individuals of Style" heritage. Jeffrey Atlas, the chairman of Atlas Citron Haligman & Bedecarre, the San Francisco agency that created the new campaign, explained that The Gap "wants to keep pushing on and try new things."[19]

BARNEYS NEW YORK

Like The Gap, Barneys New York was one of the retailing repositioning success stories of the 1980s. Under the leadership of the Pressman family, the store's founders and owners, Barneys New York evolved from a single store in New York City known for reasonably priced menswear to a global chain of high-fashion specialty apparel stores for men and women. The company opened 10 satellite stores in new markets, including southern California, Texas, and Japan, with plans for another 15 stores in additional markets and a 280,000-square-foot store on Madison Avenue in New York, destined to become its new flagship.

In the 1980s, Barneys sales quadrupled (1990 sales: $160 million), making it one of the most profitable stores in the country (1990 sales-per-square-foot: $650).[20]

The successful repositioning of Barneys was the result of a long-term strategy and skillful management by merchant/owners who understood the importance of costly intangibles in selling luxury products. The Pressmans began by gradually upgrading the quality (and prices) of their menswear, introducing more "designer" labels, from classic Savile Row manufacturers, like Kilgour French & Stanbury, to avant-garde Japanese designers, like Issey Miyake. When they introduced high-fashion apparel for women, it was a logical extension of their designer business. (Today, menswear sales still represent more than half of the company's volume, but their women's business is growing at a faster pace.[21]) The Pressmans also recognize the importance of "exclusive" merchandise not available in other stores in establishing a distinctive brand image in the overcrowded retail arena. They have consistently introduced new designers whose apparel is not carried in competitive stores, at the same time that Barneys was building up their own highly profitable private-label business (which now represents about 50 percent of their merchandise).[22]

Instead of trying to compete directly against the "uptown" specialty stores in Manhattan, like Saks Fifth Avenue and Bergdorf Goodman, the Pressmans made a virtue of their somewhat isolated "downtown" location, which contributed to the store's hip sensibility. As Gene Pressman, executive vice president, said, "There are two subcultures in New York: those who won't go below 57th Street, and downtown, which is more Bohemian and where there has been a tremendous renaissance and growth."[23] It also imbued a trip to Barneys with a special sense of occasion which encouraged purchase; in direct contrast to the ubiquitous Gap stores, one seldom dropped in to browse. There was a strong emphasis on visual design, which enhanced the appeal of the merchandise for the Alpha consumer, from the sleek, sophisticated store design by Peter Marino to the witty and whimsical store windows created by Simon Doonan, which have become a focus of the downtown arts scene, attracting the kind of attention usually reserved for gallery openings. (Mr. Doonan, Barneys' creative director, in collaboration with a variety of other designers, painters, sculptors, and photographers, has created unforgettable tableaus of everything from Nancy Reagan's White House farewell to Christmas with Tammy Faye Bakker and her giant "mascara wand" Christmas tree.) We have already discussed the impact of the innovative—and influential—advertising created by Barneys' in-house agency under the direction of Neil Kraft in repositioning the store's image (see chapter 4, Monitoring the Trendsetters). Barneys' image has been further enhanced by skillful public relations, from charitable benefits (e.g., Barneys not only sponsored Suzanne Bartsch's "Love Ball II: The Crowning Glory," a vogueing extravaganza in New York in 1991 that raised nearly $1 million for the care of AIDS patients, they later held a special auction in their flagship store for the "crowns," which had been created by the likes of Michael Graves, Francesco Clemente, and Paloma Picasso, raising an additional $150,000) to fun and imaginative store openings (e.g., to celebrate the opening of the Dallas store in 1990, guests were flown by helicopter to the empty Cotton Bowl stadium and taken by golf carts to a tent on the 30-yard line where a party was held).

Finally, we should note the Pressmans' adherence to two fundamental rules of retailing overlooked by so many of their competitors: They provide the customer with excellent service (e.g., free alterations) and they do not devalue their merchandise in the eyes of the consumer with frequent markdowns (e.g., there are basically two sales a year, at the end of each "fashion season," which are often held in a separate warehouse so that the actual stores are not tarnished by a promotional atmosphere).

LESSONS LEARNED

A successful repositioning represents a logical business evolution as we saw at Chanel, The Gap, and Barneys New York. This type of gradual change requires a long-term perspective; it also frequently requires an autocratic vision as we saw in each of the four case studies.

Sometimes new talent may be needed to effectuate the change, as Mr. Wertheimer recognized when he hired Karl Lagerfeld at Chanel or Mr. Fisher realized when he recruited Mickey Drexler to supervise the repositioning of The Gap.

The introduction of new products and new advertising campaigns can alert customers to the repositioning. At Chanel, The Gap, and Barneys New York, updated products were an integral part of the repositioning; at Absolut vodka, The Gap, and Barneys New York, distinctive advertising and a major presence in image-building magazines, from mainstream books like *Vogue* to niche ones like *Interview*, was critical in establishing a new brand identity.

Associations with the art world may enhance Alpha consumer esteem for your business. Mr. Roux says, "It's important to be associated with art in general. The artists and the people who buy art are the trendsetters in the world. Their association with Absolut sets a trend with Absolut."[24] Whether it was Absolut advertising created by artists like Andy Warhol, the inclusion of artists like Larry Rivers in The Gap "Individuals of Style" advertising campaign, the store windows at Barneys New York created by a variety of painters, photographers, and designers, or Chanel's sponsorship of *Metropolitan Home*'s showcase to benefit the Design Industries Foundation for AIDS, the response of Alpha consumers, was, in every case, extremely positive.

Philanthropic support of AIDS causes may also enhance Alpha consumer esteem for your business; Absolut, Chanel, and Barneys New York have all been prominent sponsors of fundraising events for AIDS, like Suzanne Bartsch's Love Balls.

If you are in the retailing industry, the importance of exclusive merchandise, striking visual design, artful display, and superior customer service in attracting the Alpha consumer cannot be underestimated as the success of The Gap, Barneys New York, and Chanel attests.

CHAPTER 8

REVERSE-CHIC SUCCESSES

Their general aversion to fads, and products that are self-consciously trendy, occasionally leads Alpha consumers to proletarian brands, which are valued for their integrity and lack of pretense. These products are usually inexpensive and widely distributed; they are likely to be found in blue collar homes throughout the country. They are often the leading brand within their mass market product category (e.g., Procter & Gamble's Old Spice after-shave) and sometimes almost synonymous with the category (e.g., in many circles, a beer is a "Bud"). With a few notable exceptions (e.g., the iconic advertising for Philip Morris's Marlboro cigarettes), Alphas are consumers *in spite* of the company's marketing programs; indeed, most of these companies are quite unaware of their avant-garde following. This is probably the key to their success with the Alpha consumer; a reverse-chic marketing strategy would be doomed to fail.

Alphas respect the fact that these are not aspirational purchases for *anyone*. As we noted in our discussion of Perrier (see chapter 6, Evolutionary Successes), the Alpha consumer became alienated when many people started drinking Perrier simply because it was trendy. Perrier became too closely associated with status seekers, and the Alpha consumer moved on to other bottled waters. When an Alpha consumer orders a Budweiser instead of a chic imported beer or uses Fabergé's Aqua Net hairspray instead of an expensive salon product, there is no confusion about his or her motivation because neither Budweiser nor Aqua Net would ever be misconstrued as an aspirational purchase.

It should be noted that most reverse-chic successes are very basic products that offer acceptable quality for the price, whether it is Kellogg Corn Flakes or Marlboro cigarettes. The Alpha consumer's appreciation of superior quality generally prevents him or her from compromising standards in higher-ticket categories, like automobiles, where there is a greater disparity in quality between upscale and mass market products.

Reverse-chic brands should not be confused with the occasional Alpha involvement with products that may be considered "camp" or parodies; these are usually fads that reflect the Alpha appreciation of popular culture and kitsch. When Alpha consumers serve Jello or Hostess Twinkies; wear polyester clothes; go bowling or play miniature golf; or vacation in Las Vegas, they are engaging in a form of dada consumption—the they're-so-out-they're-in syndrome—which is totally different in spirit to their loyalty to the proletarian brands they value for their honesty.

LESSONS LEARNED

You do not have to be trendy to appeal to the trendsetting consumer. Alpha loyalty to proletarian brands like Marlboro cigarettes, Budweiser beer, Old Spice after-shave, or Aqua Net hairspray is due, in part, to the fact that they are *not* trendy and would never be misconstrued as aspirational purchases.

Consistency is key to building brand equity. For example, the iconic stature of the Marlboro cigarette package and advertising imagery are more the result of consistency than distinguished design.

The implicit endorsement of influential users, from Liza Minelli to Ed McCabe, (see p. 143) has helped these brands retain their desirable identities and leadership positions in their categories.

CHAPTER 9

TOO-SOON-TO-TELL
SUCCESSES

Nike, Ben & Jerry's, Mazda Miata, and The Body Shop are products currently favored by many Alpha consumers, but it is too soon to tell whether they will become "classic" brands that enjoy long-term success. Each brand is at a critical point in its business development. Ben & Jerry's, Mazda Miata, and The Body Shop are starting to make the transition from "insider's" brands with a cult following to broader consumer acceptance; Nike has successfully made the transition. But the marketing challenge for all four brands is similar: how to broaden the appeal of their product without alienating their original consumer. Mike Rogers, chairman of Campbell-Mithun-Esty/Chicago, offers a word of caution: To keep a brand hot, "you have to find out what's driving that loyal customer—not the fad user . . . you move away from the original franchise with tremendous danger," and he warns against the "terrible temptation" to broaden a brand in an attempt to make it all things to all people.[1]

These four companies are facing many of the same issues. At Nike, Ben & Jerry's, and The Body Shop, the company's founder is still providing strategic direction and actively managing the business. However, this unique entrepreneurial vision is difficult to maintain as a company grows, and decision making must be increasingly delegated to others. At what point in its development should a company expand its original vision and recruit new talent? For example, Philip Knight, the founder and chairman of Nike, is a fanatic about running. He started Nike in 1964 with the introduction of a single Japanese running-shoe line, and a passion for running was the principal requirement for his employees. Consequently, people with little functional training ran everything from marketing to accounting. This narrow focus on runners isolated management; they lost touch with the market and ended up with 22 million pairs of unsold inventory running shoes when the running craze peaked in 1984.[2] Following this debacle, however, Mr. Knight recruited new marketing and advertising personnel; he restructured the organization with more traditional divisional management; consumer research was conducted; the company became marketing-driven. This new strategy was a significant factor in Nike's subsequent success.

Another potential danger facing these companies is the risk that they will become victims of their own success; when you are a "hot" brand, it is often difficult to resist the temptation to broaden distribution, enter new product categories, or license your name. Companies must sometimes be willing to sacrifice short-term sales gains to protect their image, which will help to ensure long-term success. Moreover, a radical departure from their heritage may diminish their credibility in the eyes of the consumer. Ben Cohen, the co-founder and chief executive officer of Ben & Jerry's Homemade Inc., explains his rationale for remaining firmly in the frozen dairy dessert category, "We feel it's really important to focus, and everything Ben & Jerry's stands for is quality . . . that you can't really be the highest product quality in a lot of different product categories. It's difficult to do, and it's difficult for the consumer to believe it. So we're just focusing on frozen dairy products."

Advertising is another critical issue. The very "public" nature of advertising can diminish the mystique of a brand that was built largely upon word-of-mouth. The challenge lies in the creation of advertising that is hip enough to maintain that insider's cachet and the brand loyalty of the Alpha consumer while making it accessible to new users. "Once it becomes another nice, advertised brand, you lose your edge," admits Tony Wright, president of McElligott Wright Morrison White, a Minneapolis advertising agency. Mr. Wright also recognizes the importance of timing: "It's very tricky. There's a point at which advertising can really drive the brand forward, and there's a point at which taking it forward into the mass market can invalidate the brand."[3]

Each of the following four companies is at a different stage in their advertising evolution. Nike has successfully made the transition to mass market advertising without alienating their Alpha consumers—serious jocks and the hip young urban blacks who set the pace in athletic footwear. Mazda Miata is moving from a print advertising strategy into television advertising. Ben & Jerry's and The Body Shop remain advertising virgins.

NIKE

Nike (1990 sales: $2.1 billion) is the leader in the $5.5-billion athletic shoe industry with 28.4 percent market share.[4] Nike's success is the result of a consistent positioning and expert marketing. Nike has always represented performance, state-of-the-art technology, and masculine appeal. This has been effectively reinforced in advertising and public relations programs targeted at the serious "jock" because the company recognizes the importance of this consumer's endorsement in maintaining a desirable brand identity in the highly competitive athletic shoe market.

In the 1980s, Nike recruited product designers from outside the shoe industry, people like architect Tinker Hatfield, to develop new technologies. Athletic shoes evolved from simple canvas footwear to high-tech fashion statements, which enabled the company to triple their price-points. (Retail prices for some Nike shoes are now $125.) The stream of new products—and corresponding price increases—contributed to the consumer's perception of quality and performance. This was reinforced by Nike's distribution channels: sporting goods stores and specialty shoe chains, like Foot Locker.

(It should be noted that Nike deviated from this strategy once in the mid-1980s with disastrous results: When the demand for running shoes leveled off in 1984, Nike started selling excess inventory to Sears and discount outlets—traditionally the last resort of the desperate. This jeopardized Nike's quality image and made it easier for Reebok to usurp its leadership position in 1988.)

Although Nike has become a major mass market advertiser, the company has always relied more on imaginative promotional techniques than on advertising to build awareness and create a distinctive brand identity; this has contributed significantly to the brand's insider's cachet. (In 1990, Nike spent $51 million on advertising—and $53 million on promotion.[5]) Nike's promotional techniques include: high school and college programs (e.g., coaches, especially basketball, are paid up to $200,000 a year to outfit their teams in Nike shoes[6]); inner city programs (e.g., Nike renovates old basketball courts and gives away samples of newly designed shoes to kids who set the trends in athletic shoes); and sponsorship of sporting events, both professional and amateur, which reinforces the close ties with athletes established in the Nike advertising featuring professional sports stars.

Nike's use of professional athlete endorsements (e.g., Michael Jordan earns $1.6 million a year endorsing Nike's Air Jordans)[7] has been successful because they are appropriate, generally exclusive, and accessible. Nike usually engages professional athletes before they achieve super stardom, so that they serve the product (not the other way around); endorsers are signed for long-term deals, so that their association with the product becomes inextricable in the minds of consumers. Moreover, Nike bypasses athletes with previous product endorsements, so there is no confusion in consumers' eyes. Finally, Nike presents the athletes in unexpected, often humorous, ways that make them more "human" and appealing. The Nike advertising agency since 1986, Wieden & Kennedy in Portland, Oregon, has consistently created highly original, witty commercials that have largely defined hip TV advertising in recent years.

We have included Nike in this discussion of "too-soon-to-tell" successes because its continued growth is by no means guaranteed. The growth of the athletic shoe market in this country (which increased from $1.5 billion in 1980 to $5.5 billion in 1990) has leveled off; in 1990, unit sales increased a mere 2.6 percent.[8] Moreover, purchase is motivated by novelty and fads, and there is little brand loyalty. In the last twenty years, the leadership position has been owned by Converse, Adidas, Nike, Reebok—

and now Nike again. Nike's long-term success will be contingent upon the development of strong brand loyalty among jocks, their Alpha consumers.

BEN & JERRY'S

Like Nike, Ben & Jerry's profited from a burgeoning product category in the 1980s: The super premium ice cream market growth was 20 percent annually. Today, it is a $2-billion category. Ben & Jerry's Homemade Inc. began in 1978 when two hippies, Ben Cohen and Jerry Greenfield, opened a single ice cream store in Vermont. The company now sells over $75 million worth of ice cream a year, and their headquarters in Waterbury, Vermont, has become the second most popular tourist attraction in the state, attracting more than 200,000 visitors a year. This cult status is the result of superior products and thoroughly unorthodox marketing.

Mr. Cohen succinctly identifies the principal factors in their success, "The first thing is the quality. The second thing is the innovative flavors. The third thing would be unusual marketing—unusual because it's honest. The fourth is probably our active concern for the community." Alpha consumers loved the rich, creamy taste and the imaginative flavors—and their names—like Heathbar Crunch and Cherry Garcia (inspired by Jerry Garcia of the Grateful Dead, the ultimate hippy band), which made their competitors, like Häagen Dazs seem boring and old-fashioned. They also responded favorably to the distinctive and funky package (with its irreverent picture of Mr. Cohen and Mr. Greenfield) and the company's marketing, from the Cowmobiles (old mobile homes painted to resemble fields of cows that traveled around, giving out ice cream) to philanthropy. The company contributes 7.5 percent of its pretax income to the Ben & Jerry's Foundation Inc., a nonprofit organization that has supported causes ranging from the preservation of the tropical rain forests to the renovation of a New York City subway station. The media coverage of Ben & Jerry's philanthropy has been far more effective in building brand awareness and establishing a favorable brand identity among Alpha consumers than advertising. As Mr. Cohen notes, "I think consumers are starting to realize that it is possible for them to vote with their pocketbook—and they can choose to support those companies which actualize values they believe in. I think that consumers are looking more and more at what a company does (or does not do) to help (or hurt) the community when they make decisions about 'what company do I like?' Some companies are out there using Michael Jackson and other performing artists or sports stars in order to get people to like them; now I think companies are starting to realize that if they can just use that $500,000 or $2 million they pay to Michael Jackson to endorse them to improve the quality of life for people in the community—by renovating parks or improving school systems—that it will go much further for them."

Like many entrepreneurial companies, Ben & Jerry's long-term growth may be limited by its founder's narrow focus. Mr. Cohen admits that his target customer is "pretty much people like myself," and he has been late in introducing certain innovations, from "lite" products to half-gallon packaging. To ensure their continued growth, the company must anticipate the tastes of a broader customer base and become more aggressive in new product development.

MAZDA MIATA

In the early 1980s Mazda Motors of America, Inc. positioned their products as the low-priced alternative to other Japanese automakers. This marketing strategy did not enhance Mazda's brand image, and sales and profitability suffered. In 1988, the company sold 250,300 cars amounting to 2.4 percent of the market—far behind its nearest Japanese competitor, Nissan, which had a 4.4 percent share.[9] At that time, George McCabe, the company's newly appointed group vice president of sales and marketing, recognized that his "chief task is creating an image . . . a mystique."[10] The introduction of the Miata model in 1989, a moderately priced version of the classic British roadster convertible, was the first step in the company's new marketing strategy. The Miata was an immediate sensation among Alpha consumers. Sales amounted to 23,052 units in only six months on the market,[11] its entire allotment for the year. Film director Stephen Spielberg presented four of them at a "wrap" celebration to Richard Dreyfuss, Holly Hunter, John Goodman, and Brad Johnson, the stars of his movie *Always*. Mazda dealers reported that customers were willing to pay them thousands of dollars in bribes simply to hold the first places in lines for the new models. Classified ads on both coasts began appearing, with owners offering to sell their slightly used Miatas for $10,000 above the original sticker price.[12] Most important, the introduction of the Miata successfully established a new image for the company. Jan Thompson, vice president of advertising, noted that "The Miata is an incredible halo for us,"[13] and *Advertising Age* announced that Mazda "had entered the year recognized as a marketer of price/value, low-cost cars and trucks" and "exited as a marketer of premium-quality vehicles."

The genesis of the Miata is an inspired example of corporate risk-taking. Kenichi Yamamoto, Mazda's chairman, wanted to create an image-building product that was tailored for the American market; in 1981, Mr. Yamamoto departed from traditional Mazda product development procedures and hired an American automotive journalist, Robert Hall, as a product planner in the company's planning studio in Irvine, California. The Miata is essentially Mr. Hall's "dream machine" inspired by his love of British sports car convertibles like the Triumph Spitfire. Mr. Hall was guided by his instincts; he admits that "We hadn't done focus groups or market studies."[14] Rod Bymaster, the manager of sport cars, added, "Management here and in Japan had to be sold on introducing a car that had no real competition . . . that was based mostly on hunches."[15] Although Mazda knew that the number of potential buyers for a sporty two-passenger convertible would be relatively few compared to the market for a family sedan, they also recognized the importance of targeting Alpha consumers in establishing a desirable corporate identity. Mr. Bymaster explained their rationale in adopting a narrow niche marketing strategy: "By trying to hit a huge group, you project a broad fuzzy image that few really identify with."

Alpha consumers did identify with the Miata. They loved the uniqueness and the associations with British celluloid heroes of the 1960s, like Emma Peel from "The Avengers" and James

Bond. They responded favorably to the simplicity of the concept; for example, the fact that the Miata was available in only three basic colors—red, white and mariner blue—was considered an asset with the implications that the car was not for everyone. With a base price of $13,800, Alphas appreciated the quality and value that Miata offered and the sense that it would not be confused with the more expensive, aspirational cars, like BMWs, that had come to be too narrowly associated with the nouveau riche. Finally, Alphas responded to the playfulness that Miata represented; in many ways, it was a toy for adults—somewhat impractical but fun. The enthusiastic endorsement of the trade press—*Road & Track* magazine named the Miata one of the five best cars in the world judged by design, durability/reliability, entertainment, performance, and value and favorably compared the Miata to the Ferrari Testarossa, which costs $126,000 more—provided "reassurance" (if any was required) and contributed significantly to the tremendous consumer buzz that the Miata generated.

The marketing challenge now facing Mazda is how to turn the Miata into a classic car synonymous with the affordable two-seater convertible category it reinvented. The company will have to resist the temptation to flood the market while the brand is hot; it is currently the only car that does not require a dealer's rebate, and Mazda should not jeopardize that enviable position with discounting. They must also resist the temptation to follow a strategy of forced obsolescence; future models should maintain the stylistic heritage of the original version, in much the same way that Harley-Davidson maintains the heritage of their "Hogs." The customer base should be expanded to include more women and older consumers with a youthful spirit. (Many baby boomers will be ready to trade in their family-sized sedans and station wagons for something that is fun to drive when their children leave home; affluent older consumers will be willing to purchase a Miata as a second or third car.) However, Mazda must protect the sporty masculine image that Miata enjoys to ensure the continued patronage of its Alpha consumers—men who are fanatics about sports cars.

THE BODY SHOP

The Body Shop is the first cosmetics company to capitalize on two trends pioneered by Alpha consumers: environmental marketing and specialty store distribution. The British-based company began in 1976 as a retailer of cosmetics and toiletries formulated with natural ingredients; as the company grew, this eco-awareness positioning has been expanded to include a ban on animal testing, recycling programs for its customers, and social action campaigns. Today, The Body Shop is a $200-million-a-year company with more than 500 shops throughout the world.[16] The company entered the U.S. market in 1988 with 14 stores on the East Coast. By 1990, there were 34 U.S. stores, which generated sales of $20 million.[17] In the next 10 years, the company plans to open 1,000 stores across the country, according to Anita Roddick, the founder and managing director.[18]

Alpha consumers in this country responded to The Body Shop's environmental positioning, seductive merchandising, and novelty. The Body Shops are in many ways the antithesis of the large department stores and drug stores where most consumers purchase their cosmetics and toiletries. They are small, highly focused, and user-friendly with open product displays. They are decorated a dark green inside and out, which reinforces their environmental positioning and provides a visually striking background for their brilliantly colored soaps and beribboned hampers of gels and shampoos. Marketing is based on environmentalism and appealing natural "ingredient stories" like Cucumber Cleansing Milk and Pineapple Facial Wash; there is a refreshing lack of extravagant product performance claims. Says Miss Roddick: "We don't mention the word 'beauty,' we don't make promises of any kind, other than to say that our stuff will clean and protect your hair and skin, amen."[19] The sales approach is decidedly soft sell; many of the people who work in the stores are idealistic young people who identify with the company's environmentalism, which enables them to effectively "bond" with their customers (many of whom are also idealistic young people). There is no fragrance "spritzing," promotional gimmicks like "purchase-with-purchase" premiums, or photographs of glamorous models. ("We don't have photographic images. Our concept of beauty is Mother Teresa, not some bimbo or Princess Diana or whomever by the grace of God was given a couple of high cheekbones," explains Miss Roddick.[20]) As we noted, The Body Shop does not advertise, which has enhanced the credibility of its anticommercial stance and contributed to its insider's cachet; its success so far has been due to word-of-mouth and the sales acumen of each franchisee.

Unfortunately, product quality is uneven. Miss Roddick is clearly more involved with the environmental and social causes her financial success (her personal worth exceeds $200 million)[21] has enabled her to pursue than with the basics of her business. ("Look", she says, "I'm sorry, but I can't talk about moisturizer as if it was the body and blood of Jesus Christ."[22]) Despite the appeal of The Body Shop's environmentalism, merchandising, and accessible price-points (the average purchase ranges from $12 to $14), Alpha consumers have found the overall product quality unacceptable; repurchase is generally limited to one or two formulations that this consumer has deemed satisfactory. The Body Shop has benefited considerably from its lack of competition. As other companies enter the market with superior "natural" products, there is likely to be further erosion of Alpha brand loyalty unless the company upgrades the quality of its formulations (which must perform at least as well as mass market products). And with the growing consumer awareness of specious "green marketing" as every company jumps on the environmental bandwagon, The Body Shop will have to become more aggressively eco-aware or risk hypocrisy—and consumer alienation. For example, the company should address its use of plastic packaging and cellowrap. Finally, The Body Shop will have to maintain stricter control of its American franchisees where the service is as uneven as the product quality.

LESSONS LEARNED

Most businesses in growth categories must successfully reach Alphas because these pioneering consumers are characteristically the most receptive to new types of products. High-tech athletic shoes, premium ice cream, and natural cosmetics were burgeoning categories in the 1980s; the respective successes of Nike, Ben & Jerry's, and The Body Shop were largely the result of skillful Alpha target marketing. The continued success of these companies will be contingent upon retaining the brand loyalty of their Alpha franchise while broadening their customer base, as Nike has done.

To successfully make the transition from a highly focused, entrepreneurial business to a diversified enterprise with long-term growth potential, most companies must expand the founder's original vision and become consumer-driven. This is one of the critical issues now facing Ben & Jerry's and The Body Shop.

The involvement of "outsiders" in the product development process may lead to breakthrough advances, as Nike demonstrated when it hired a trained architect, Tucker Hatfield, to design athletic shoes and Mazda proved when it engaged an automotive journalist, Robert Hall, to create the Miata.

Businesses built upon word-of-mouth must approach advertising with caution because the very public nature of advertising can undermine the insider's cachet that was a critical factor in their initial success. But Nike has proven that it is possible to venture into mass market advertising without invalidating the brand in the eyes of the Alpha consumer.

CHAPTER 10

SHORT-TERM SUCCESSES

Some new products initially endorsed by Alpha consumers are adopted so quickly by the mainstream that they create the sensation of a fad, something the highly independent Alpha consumer tries to avoid. Alphas are particularly sensitive to businesses with hip aspirations, whether it involves a "boutique" beer like Corona or a "downtown" magazine like *Spy* or a high-fashion watch like Swatch; these are likely to pass from chic to passé almost overnight. The sudden and seemingly ubiquitous appearance of these new products, and the early defection by the Alpha consumer, told the mainstream that these were fads, and they, too, began to move on, severely curtailing the product's life cycle. Ultimately, no one wants to be associated with a fad.

CORONA BEER

In the mid-1980s Corona Extra Mexican beer was "hot." Its success was due to its novelty; its distinctive, clear, long-necked bottle; the fact that it was imported but tasted like traditional American brews, assuring widespread consumer acceptance; distribution in trendy bars and restaurants; the custom of adding a sliver of lime, which made it appear particularly exotic; its early adoption in California (often a harbinger of trends); and the lack of significant advertising in an advertising-driven category, which only enhanced its insider's cachet. In 1987, Barton Beers Ltd. in Chicago, which imports Corona beer from Mexico, sold 22.5 million cases.[1]

However, by 1990, sales in the United States had dropped

to 16 million cases according to Impact, a beverage industry publication; the decline is likely to continue as more mainstream consumers discover that Corona is no longer fashionable. The demise of Corona beer was the result of its fad perception, increasing competition from domestic beer makers in the form of new products, such as dry beers, and a lack of marketing expertise. When Barton Beers Ltd. started advertising Corona in 1988, it was already too late; the momentum was gone. Mike Rogers, chairman of Campbell-Mithun-Esty Advertising in Chicago, which won the account that year, acknowledged, "We came in while it was on the express train to hell."[2] The Corona business was further weakened by the company's failure to introduce timely line extensions (a light beer was introduced in 1989) and by image-destructive devices designed to increase revenues, like 12-packs.

SWATCH WATCH

The introduction of the Swatch watch in 1983 revolutionized the watch industry. In many ways, Swatch represented a negation of all the industry's traditional concepts. It was positioned as an inexpensive fashion accessory, not fine jewelry, and was sold in department stores, not jewelers. With the built-in obsolescence characteristic of fashion products, there were seasonal collections of new models. They could not be opened or repaired—they had to be discarded if malfunctioning. This heretical approach was reinforced with marketing and advertising programs that were decidedly hip at the time. Swatch was one of the first companies to adopt an MTV approach to advertising, in print as well as broadcast. Bold graphics consistent with the product design and "short takes" characterized the Swatch advertising, which changed constantly. TV commercials frequently featured performers, like The Fat Boys, whose concert tours were sponsored by Swatch. Moreover, the Swatch "sell" was always relatively subtle and unorthodox. At Swatch-sponsored concerts, for example, there were two 6-foot Swatch watch replicas on opposite sides of the stage; spotlights hit the replicas 30 seconds before the show began, counting down the last moments in a crescendo of "Swatch ticking" from the sound system. The performers always wore Swatch watches—often several at the same time—which established a fad among teenagers. (Alannah Currie of The Thompson Twins wore a coat lined with 100 Swatch watches, but that was beyond the budget of most young people.) In its selection of sponsorships and promotions, Swatch was consistently on the newest wave, whether it was breakdancing in 1984 or rap music in 1985.

Initially, Alpha consumers responded favorably to the Swatch watch phenomenon; they liked the stylish designs, the renegade appeal of disposable watches, and the hip sensibility of the company's marketing programs. Worldwide unit sales of Swatch watches increased from 400,000 in 1983 to 12.8 million in 1986 before demand began to decline. (Despite substantial investment spending in Swatch watch, its success enabled the parent company SMH, a subsidiary of Asuag-SSIH, a Swiss consortium, to improve its bottom line from a loss of $129 million in 1983 to profits of $48 million in 1986.[3]) However, when Swatch watches became a "cult" product among teenagers, Alpha consumers began to lose interest. Today, kids represent the primary market for Swatch watches. According to Richard Shriner, former vice president of marketing, "We discovered that the market for fashion watches had become very segmented, and our strength lay with the children and young teen markets."[4]

SPY MAGAZINE

When the first issue of *Spy* magazine appeared in October 1986, Alpha consumers appreciated its antiestablishment sensibility, even if the humor was more often sophomoric than genuinely satirical. They were entertained by the devices designed to establish an insider's cachet for the magazine, from the origin of the title (named for the unscrupulous magazine that employed Jimmy Stewart in the 1940 film *The Philadelphia Story*) to the development of a private language for familiar behavior (e.g., "silly gestures" was *Spy* talk for "sexual intercourse"). Alpha consumers in Manhattan were also amused by the pains taken by the publishers to create a hip identity for the magazine, from their offices in the Puck Building in Soho to the prepublication lunches for writers and editors at Mare Chiaro, an old-fashioned Italian "social club" on Mulberry Street, to the huge promotional parties held at clubs like The Tunnel.

However, the Alpha reader soon tired of *Spy*, and the magazine received a flood of cancellations.[5] Some Alpha readers objected to the shameless "borrowing" from British magazines (e.g., the "Make-Believe Mailbag," which offered Nancy Reagan's letters to Betsy Bloomingdale, was based on the "Dear Bill" correspondence between Margaret Thatcher's husband and a fellow clubman in *Private Eye*). Others were bored by the one-note editorial, which never evolved beyond derision and became all too predictable. Others resented the magazine's efforts to generate publicity (and advertising dollars) by writing constantly about the media; when *Spy* was featured in mainstream media like *USA Today* and "Live at Five" with gossip columnist Liz Smith (a local NBC television news program in New York), it lost its insider's cachet and started attracting outsiders with hip aspirations. Today, the outsiders are discovering that *Spy* is no longer in. Circulation has dropped 17 percent below the figure of 130,000 paid copies guaranteed to advertisers,[6] and the desperate publishers have been distributing free copies in New York apartment building lobbies in an effort to increase circulation—an ill-conceived ploy that has further diminished the magazine's mystique. Moreover, *Spy* has lost much of its appeal for media buyers. "*Spy* symbolized the yuppie era and now that's over," said Claude Fromm, executive vice president/media director at TBWA, the agency for one of *Spy*'s most important advertisers, Absolut vodka. "There's a lot of negativism within the advertising community associated with *Spy*, and that will be hard to turn around."[7] Advertising pages have declined 34 percent in the past two years, from 620 pages in 1988 to 412 pages in 1990.[8] Although British advertising agency founder Charles Saatchi and three other European investors acquired a 70 percent interest in *Spy* in December 1990 for $4 million (reportedly attributed to Mr. Saatchi's idiosyncratic affinity for the magazine and its British counterpart *Private Eye*),[9] it remains to be seen whether an infusion of capital to promote the magazine can resurrect it.

TRIVIAL PURSUIT

When Trivial Pursuit, a board game that capitalized on consumers' fascination with minutiae, was introduced in the United States in 1983, it became an overnight sensation among many Alphas. With their knowledge and appreciation of popular culture, many Alphas were highly proficient players, and their social orientation made them very receptive to the novelty of an adult board game. In the summer of 1983, Trivial Pursuit was an after-dinner ritual in many vacation homes throughout the country. The appeal of Trivial Pursuit was further enhanced by its insider's cachet (it was unadvertised) and by its lack of availability (a classic example of scarcity only heightening demand).

Although Trivial Pursuit had been successfully introduced in Canada in 1982, U.S. distributer Selchow & Righter, a $40-million company built on the steady success of Scrabble and Parcheesi, had not anticipated its phenomenal popularity in the United States, and there were frequent out-of-stock periods in 1983. But by 1984, Selchow & Righter had engaged five additional outside manufacturers to handle production. Moreover, the mainstream had discovered Trivial Pursuit. Industry analysts estimated that Trivial Pursuit generated $660 million in retail sales in 1984, double that of *all* board games the prior year.[10] Selchow & Righter sales increased tenfold to more than $400 million.[11]

However, by 1984, Alpha consumers had begun to lose interest in Trivial Pursuit. There were several reasons for the Alpha defection. First of all, the game was too limiting. It lacked the tactical maneuvers and psychological challenge of poker or bridge; once you knew the questions and answers, it became very routine (and the line extensions such as the Baby Boomer Edition were disappointing). Second, Trivial Pursuit became so trendy that it was unable to transcend a dangerous fad perception. Third, the company's saturation strategy backfired: The game, which usually retailed for about $30, started showing up in discount outlets for little more than the $19 wholesale price, seriously damaging its upscale image and undermining its retail relationships. "It's ironic that after having to beg to get stock for nine months the market is suddenly flooded with the stuff," said F.A.O. Schwarz' senior buyer Ian McDermott. "It leaves a rather bad taste in one's mouth."[12] By 1990, annual unit sales of Trivial Pursuit had declined to less than 300,000 games, while other adult games, like Milton Bradley's Scattergories sold 1.8 million units.[13]

LESSONS LEARNED

Businesses with successful, but limited potential, products must diversify *before* sales peak and the brand begins to lose momentum. Corona beer, Swatch watch, and Trivial Pursuit failed to recognize the inherent limitations of their products; by the time they embarked on diversification strategies, it was too late.

Sometimes scarcity can create a heightened sense of demand that cannot realistically be sustained; when Corona beer, Swatch watch, and Trivial Pursuit became widely available, they lost much of their allure.

No business can afford to alienate the trade; when Trivial Pursuit started appearing in discount outlets and free copies of *Spy* magazine materialized in apartment building lobbies, each seriously jeopardized its trade support—retailers in the case of Trivial Pursuit, and advertisers in the case of *Spy*.

Overexposure in the media can contribute to a dangerous fad perception. For example, the media obsession with *Spy* and Trivial Pursuit (due in part to the conspicuous media references included in each of those products) undermined their viability.

Many businesses lack the experience to skillfully maximize the potential of a fad product. Barton Beers Ltd. and Selchow & Righter were clearly unprepared for the phenomenal success of Corona beer and Trivial Pursuit, respectively; the companies should have sought marketing assistance, in the form of new personnel or outside experts, people with an understanding of the dynamics involved.

CHAPTER 11

MISSED OPPORTUNITIES

There are some businesses that Alpha consumers would like to patronize because they correspond to certain Alpha values, but the company's marketing program makes this impossible. In other words, a missed opportunity. Sometimes the Alpha consumer is a former user whose brand loyalty was jeopardized by uneven quality control or a decline in product quality; this was the case with the Izod Lacoste polo shirt. Other times the erosion of Alpha brand loyalty was due to the manufacturer's failure to keep up with technical advancements in the industry. This was the case with Tenax hair fixative: When competitors introduced superior product formulations, the Alpha customer was forced to change brands. Sometimes unrealistically high price-points prevented the Alpha consumer from becoming a customer, as was the case with the ultrahip fashions of Stephen Sprouse: Club kids loved the designs, but they could not afford them. Sometimes the products and price-points were on target, but the company's marketing and promotion alienated the Alpha consumer. This was the case with Avon Products: The Alpha consumer simply could not relate to the presentation of the products in the Avon campaign brochures. Finally, some businesses fail to capitalize on social trends that dictate changes in consumers' life-styles and purchase behavior; this was the case with Sears, Roebuck: As consumers gradually rejected the conspicuous consumption and designer brand orientation of the 1980s and returned to more traditional American values with an emphasis on family and home, many were also ready to "return" to Sears, but the company's inconsistency—in merchandising, product quality, pricing, and marketing—kept them away. (It is no coincidence that

Wal-Mart has surpassed Sears as the country's leading retailer while Bloomingdale's is in Chapter 11). In this chapter, we briefly examine four businesses that illustrate different types of "missed opportunities."

AVON PRODUCTS

Several trends in the marketplace should have predisposed Alpha consumers to purchasing cosmetics and toiletries from Avon Products. First, ordering by phone and home delivery has become second nature for these busy consumers who do not particularly enjoy shopping. Second, the decline in the level of service provided in department store cosmetics departments and in drug stores is another incentive to order by phone or mail. Third, a growing appreciation of value and a resistance to the exorbitant price increases in recent years of upscale cosmetics brands should enhance the appeal of Avon's products, which offer very acceptable quality for the price and a 100 percent unconditional customer satisfaction guarantee. Finally, the general nature of Alpha purchase behavior—decisive, brand loyal, impervious to promotional gimmicks—should work to Avon's advantage.

Unfortunately, Alpha consumers, with a keen sense of visual style, cannot relate to the presentation of the products in the Avon campaign brochures, which are supremely distasteful to them—poorly designed, claustrophobic, and cheaply printed. If Avon marketing management believed that more stylish sales materials might alienate their existing consumer franchise, a debatable proposition, they should have developed a niche marketing strategy that included separate brochures targeted at more sophisticated women. (The median age of the Avon customer is 45 with average annual income below $30,000 and 14 percent of American women represent one-third of its customer base.[1]) This would have attracted influential new users who would have updated the company's tarnished image at the same time they generated incremental sales.

STEPHEN SPROUSE

Unlike Avon Products, Stephen Sprouse cannot be accused of neglecting the Alpha consumer. Indeed, Mr. Sprouse was idolized by Alpha consumers in the 1980s. The first American fashion designer to draw his inspiration from the street, the punk scene, and the 1960s, his first collection in 1983 of chemises and separates redolent of the 1960s but printed or painted in graffitilike patterns or sequined and shaded in brilliant hues was an immediate sensation. Publications ranging from *Vogue* to underground British magazines presented Mr. Sprouse as the rock star of American fashion. His stature was further enhanced by his impeccably hip credentials: He was a regular fixture on the CBGB and Rock Hotel hard-core scene, so his fashions were not perceived as imitations of the club scene designed by an outsider. He had made clothes for Debbie Harry in her Blondie days (long before Madonna appeared on the scene); later customers included other rock stars, like Mick Jagger. When he presented his fashion shows at the Ritz, a cavernous club in New York known for its avant-garde bands, thousands of club kids would attempt to get in. He was also an artist and part of the Andy Warhol set. (He painted things like blown-up pictures of Patty Hearst taken from the cover of the *New York Post*.) Last, but not least, Mr. Sprouse had all of the "right" connections within the fashion world. He had worked for Halston during his peak in the 1970s. He was a protégée of the late Kizia Keeble Duka, the founder of Keeble Duka Cavillo, the most powerful public relations firm in the American fashion industry. He designed the wedding dress of Elizabeth Saltzman for the Seventh Avenue wedding of the year in 1987. (Miss Saltzman is a fashion editor at *Vogue*; her mother Ellin is the senior vice president of fashion direction at Macy's.) His clothes were carried in trendy stores like Bloomingdale's and later in his own boutique in Soho, which defined hip merchandising at the time (e.g., mannequins in contorted dance positions in front of double-sided video screens playing continuous rock videos; black dressing room curtains printed with images taken from albums by Jim Morrison and The Sex Pistols; a polaroid shot of Sid Vicious tacked into the frame of a wall mirror). Although it would appear that Mr. Sprouse could have writ-

ten the book on targeting the trendsetting consumer, he overlooked one fundamental fact: the hip are often un-rich. Most of
the young people who loved his clothes could not afford them.
Retail prices ranged from $21 for a T-Shirt to $3,500 for a black
jersey dress covered with safety pins. And many of his "looks"
were a bit too easy to duplicate on your own. (Any girl with a
little black dress and a thousand safety pins—and a lot of pa-
tience—could create her own Sprouse look for a fraction of the
cost.) Unfortunately, Mr. Sprouse went out of business while his
imitators, who offered lower-priced versions of his designs, pros-
pered.

TENAX HAIR FIXATIVE

In the early 1980s, Alphas were the first people in this country
to adopt some of the new high-concept hairstyles that had orig-
inated in Europe, from sculptural punk styles to the urbane
slicked-back look. Styling gels were the key to achieving these
new looks—and Tenax was the brand of choice. (In Julia Phillips's memoir of Hollywood in the 1970s and 1980s, *You'll Never
Eat Lunch In This Town Again*, the author's collection of haircare products in her bathroom provided her with a chronicle of
those years: "There were the Tenax from her Jose-Eber-period,
the Kamikaze products from her Peter Nagai period. . . ."[2])

Tenax had all the earmarks of a classic Alpha marketing
success story. It was imported from France. The packaging was
very distinctive and upscale—a metal tube that recalled painters'
pigments, unusual green/purple/white graphics, copy in French
and English, the company's Faubourg Saint Honore address in
Paris. It was first discovered by many Alphas on European trips
(including lots of fashion stylists and models), which imbued it
with a certain mystique. There was no advertising or promotion;
awareness was built entirely on word-of-mouth, further enhanc-
ing its insider's cachet. Finally, it pioneered the designer hair
gel category in this country, where the only competition at the
time were old-fashioned products, like Gillette's Dippity-Do.

However, the product formulation was not entirely satisfactory. It frequently "flaked" or left the hair very dry. As the main-

stream gradually discovered styling gels, competitive manufacturers introduced superior products. When Tenax (distributed in this country by Excalibur Inc.) failed to keep pace with technical advancements in the marketplace, the Alpha consumer—reluctantly—changed brands.

IZOD LACOSTE

For nearly 50 years, the Izod Lacoste polo shirt, first marketed in 1933 by French tennis player Rene Lacoste, was favored by many Alpha consumers. Like Levi 501 jeans, the Izod Lacoste polo shirt with its distinctive styling (e.g., the extended shirttail in back) and alligator emblem was considered authentic; other polo shirts were imitations. Of course, many Alphas also responded favorably to the product's superior quality; natural fibers; the French heritage and sizing; and the brand's insider's cachet, from the Cote d'Azur to Martha's Vineyard.

Two developments contributed to the demise of Izod Lacoste. General Mills acquired the company in 1969, and the brand became a mainstream fashion fad in the early 1980s when the classic preppy look achieved broad popularity. Sales nearly doubled between 1979 and 1982 before they peaked at $400 million in 1982.[3] Alpha consumers did not mind that the mainstream had temporarily confiscated their polo shirt. As Jane Evans, the former executive vice president of the General Mills fashion group pointed out, "I think it's important to remember that fashion came to Izod. It was not because of anything we did as far as changing the shirt."[4] Alpha consumers recognized that the mainstream would soon move on to something else (in this case, the more expensive copies of the Izod Lacoste polo shirt that were introduced by fashion designers like Ralph Lauren), and they would have remained loyal to Izod Lacoste, if General Mills had permitted it. However, the company did not understand the dynamics of the fashion business. As Miss Evans acknowledged, "All of a sudden we were a fashion line. We didn't understand the implications of that."[5] To meet increased demand, the company sacrificed strict quality control. When the fad customer moved on in 1984 and 1985, the company was left with huge obsolete inventories, which appeared in discount outlets, further damaging its quality image and ruining its relationships with its upscale retailers who drastically reduced its selling space in their stores. As was the case with Tenax, the company literally drove the Alpha consumer away.

In 1985, General Mills sold Izod Lacoste to Crystal Brands (1990 sales: approximately $870 million),[6] a conglomerate of apparel and costume jewelry companies better suited to managing the business. Although Crystal Brands has improved quality control, substantially reduced distribution, and established Izod Lacoste boutiques in 150 department stores, sales continue to decline.

LESSONS LEARNED

No business can afford to take the Alpha consumer's patronage for granted. Uneven quality control (Izod Lacoste) or the introduction of superior competitive products (Tenax), discounting (Izod Lacoste), or unrealistically high price-points (Stephen Sprouse) can all jeopardize Alpha brand loyalty.

Corporate owners should resist the temptation to interfere in the management of acquisitions that represent new businesses; the demise of Izod Lacoste was largely attributable to mismanagement by General Mills who did not understand the dynamics of the fashion industry.

If you are not attracting any Alpha consumers, it is very difficult to maintain a desirable brand identity; Avon's tarnished image in the image-driven cosmetics industry is partly the result of the company's failure to target Alpha consumers.

PART III

MARKETING GUIDELINES

Based upon the psychographic profile of the Alpha consumer and the lessons learned from the case studies, in the chapters in Part 3 we present what we believe to be general marketing guidelines for targeting the influential Alpha buyer. The points covered are summarized as follows:

CHAPTER 12: STRATEGIC PLANNING

How to determine the role of the Alpha consumer in your industry; the strategic decision to target Alpha consumers for market development.

Self-evaluation; identifying your strengths and weaknesses from the perspective of the Alpha consumer.

The strategic implications and opportunities involved in product repositioning, product improvement, line extensions, new brands, subsidiaries, acquisitions, and licensing.

CHAPTER 13: SEMIOTICS

The importance of semiotics in targeting Alpha consumers; examples of messages conveyed by various corporate and marketing semiotics.

Corporate semiotics including heritage, ownership, location, offices, stationary, and management policies.

Marketing semiotics including product quality, name, positioning, pricing, distribution, merchandising, customer service, public relations, advertising, and promotion.

CHAPTER 14: VISUAL DESIGN

The role of visual design in Alpha purchase motivation; appealing to the Alpha visual sensibility.

Creative procedures; mnemonics; product and package design; environmental design and display.

CHAPTER 15: DISTRIBUTION AND LOCATION

The company-that-you-keep factor; how to determine the distribution channels or locations that will maximize your market potential; how to identify the up-and-coming neighborhoods to which many Alpha consumers gravitate; the implications of limited versus broad distribution.

CHAPTER 16: CUSTOMER SERVICE

Making a statement about your identity; creating an ambience that will stimulate purchase; hiring, training and motivating sales personnel; evaluating customer service efficacy.

CHAPTER 17: DIRECT MARKETING

How to maximize the efficiency of direct marketing; how to determine when direct marketing is appropriate (and when it is inappropriate).

Direct mail: visual design/sales copy; frequency; incentives; catalogs and omnibus mailings.

Telemarketing: toll-free 800 numbers; 900 numbers; staffing; unsolicited telemarketing appeals.

CHAPTER 18: PUBLIC RELATIONS

How to capitalize on the endorsement of Alpha consumers; how to maximize the public relations potential of your employees; how to identify the most influential media.

New business/new product introduction strategies: targeted Alpha campaign; slow build; media blitz; international approach.

Maintaining top-of-mind awareness; philanthropy; sponsorships; product placement.

CHAPTER 19: ADVERTISING

How to determine whether (or not) you should advertise based on an evaluation of the purchase behavior of the Alpha consumer, the nature of your industry, and your strategic objectives.

Developing a creative platform that corresponds to the core values of the Alpha consumer: information, cosmopolitanism, communication, originality, involvement, identity, and self-sufficiency; the role of spokespersons, testimonials, humor, comparative advertising, and aspirational advertising.

Media planning: print; broadcast; outdoor.

CHAPTER 20: PROMOTION

The advantages and risks involved in promotion; creating an effective promotional program; sampling and trial; frequency programs; special offers; special events; cross promotions and tie-ins; price promotions; coupons; premiums; contests and sweepstakes.

CHAPTER 21: GREEN MARKETING

Our definition of green marketing; implications and opportunities for marketers and advertisers in the 1990s; long-term stra-

tegic planning; short-term marketing and promotional techniques.

CHAPTER 12

STRATEGIC PLANNING

No business can afford to ignore the Alpha, or trendsetting, consumer. With slower growth projected in most industries in the near future, the key to increasing sales and profitablity will be innovation and new products. As pioneers, Alpha consumers will play a critical role. However, the strategic decision to target these influential consumers for business development should be based on an understanding of their purchase behavior, the dynamics of trends within your industry, and a candid assessment of your corporate identity. You must first determine whether Alpha consumers represent a potential market for your product or service. If they do, you must try to bring their value system into the marketplace as we observed in the case histories of the companies who successfully reached this consumer. If Alphas are unlikely to patronize your business because it cannot correspond to their values, you should try to monitor these trendsetting consumers and anticipate their influence on your regular customer franchise, so that you may plan your marketing strategy accordingly. As we saw, this was the case with the fast-food restaurant industry (p. 28). Sometimes marketers have hip aspirations for their businesses that are based more in fantasy than reality; they should resist the temptation to target the relatively glamorous Alpha consumer because they will invariably fail. The Alpha consumer's pursuit of information and keen sensitivity to semiotics (see chapter 13, Semiotics) will always enable him or her to detect inconsistencies in your identity; you are more likely to appeal to this consumer if you pursue a marketing strategy based on an understanding of who you are, not necessarily who you would like to be.

This kind of understanding requires extensive self-examination and a realistic assessment of your strengths and weaknesses. You may find it useful to engage outside consultants who bring an independent perspective and objectivity to the process. Or you may want to conduct a brand identity audit to determine how consumers perceive you. But your marketing strategy should reflect the type of singular vision we observed in the management of the successful companies we studied, whether they were giant corporations, like American Express or Sony, or entrepreneurial ventures, like Ben & Jerry's Homemade Inc. or The Body Shop. It should be noted that many of these companies are privately held (e.g., Chanel, Barneys New York) or actively managed by the founder (e.g., Philip Knight at Nike, Donald Fisher at The Gap) or people who are genuine "users" or "believers" in the uniqueness of their products (e.g., Vaughn Beals at Harley-Davidson, Michel Roux at Carillon Importers). This type of commitment permeates their marketing strategy and is an intrinsic part of their success.

The rationale for targeted Alpha marketing may vary. Companies with existing businesses may want to integrate these influential consumers as a critical niche in maintaining a desirable brand identity in the eyes of the mainstream. For example, we saw how Nike targets young urban blacks although 87 percent of its domestic athletic shoes are sold to whites who strive to imitate black athletes.[1] Small businesses with limited financial resources may want to target these independent consumers who are less responsive than the mainstream to expensive advertising and promotional programs. New businesses with a long-term perspective may want initially to target Alpha consumers exclusively to develop a sense of "ownership" and brand loyalty that will assure a long product life cycle. This type of slow build based on word-of-mouth usually takes several years, but it will prevent the perception of a fad, which always contributes to a product's premature demise. Finally, new businesses may want to target Alpha consumers to create a hip identity that will attract mainstream consumers with hip aspirations. For example, in the highly evanescent world of clubs in Manhattan where three or four years is considered longevity, the initial endorsement of the Alpha consumer is critical. As Michael Musto, who covers nightlife for the *Village Voice*, notes, "A really smart club owner—if he wants to be in it for the duration—will use the trendy crowd (basically the complimentary crowd) as a way to get paying customers. And eventually the paying customers will become the dominant crowd as the trendy crowd moves on. You can stop being the hot fabulous place and just be a place people go to."

In targeting Alpha consumers, marketers should rely more on psychographics than demographics. Since Alphas represent only 5 percent of the population, quantitative market research is almost impossible to obtain. Quantitative research is only valid for the mainstream, and marketers should recognize the risk inherent in mainstream consumer research. As Chris Brick, the owner of bbc, an avante-garde clothing store in Manhattan's East Village modeled after Demob in London, noted, "New things always look wrong—some people get it and some don't." And mainstream consumers don't get it. Consequently, broad-based market research will generally "kill" genuine innovation. Alphas, on the other hand, with their superior conceptual skills, independence, and sense of adventure can be a valuable resource in directional consumer research, from new product ideation to advertising evaluation. Some marketers may want to involve appropriate "professional" Alphas such as chefs, hairdressers, photographers, or athletes, in their product development process; this may lead to a superior product and generate public relations opportunities at the same time. (See chapter 18, Public Relations.)

In the identification of their strengths and weaknesses, companies must determine whether they have the correct personnel to execute an Alpha target marketing strategy. Sometimes new talent may be required, as we saw in the successful repositioning of Chanel or the development of the Mazda Miata. Sometimes companies may find it instructive to play a hypothetical game as they formulate an Alpha target marketing strategy: First, identify successful Alpha marketers in your industry or a related business; then try to anticipate what they would do if they were in your position. For example, if you are involved in:

Electronics	"Think"	Sony
Women's Fashions	"Think"	Chanel

Sporting Goods	"Think"	Nike
Specialty Retailing	"Think"	The Gap
Restaurants	"Think"	Wolfgang Puck
Hotels	"Think"	Ian Schrager

As you consider your strategic options, try to keep the values of the Alpha consumer foremost because ultimately it is the consumer who will determine whether you succeed or fail. Do not allow trade considerations to dictate your strategy. For example, we have seen the danger of discounting in image-driven categories; do not distribute your product in retail channels where this will occur. Be willing to sacrifice short-term sales gains to protect your image. Consider the general implications of the following strategies from the perspective of the Alpha consumer.

PRODUCT REPOSITIONING

The repositioning should represent a logical transition or evolution, as we observed in the successful repositioning of Chanel and The Gap. If the repositioning is too abrupt or departs radically from your heritage, it will destroy your credibility. For example, *Details* magazine lost most of its Alpha readership in 1990 when it changed from a funky, downtown magazine to a sleek and pretentious "men's" book. ("From now on, *Details* will be slanted toward men: men's fashion, men's style, men's interests.") One Alpha reader's assessment of the repositioning: "Yes, it's true that there is something out there with the name *Details* on it, but a new regime took over and turned it into one of those magazines where you can virtually see the wheels turning in the editors' brains as they try desperately, as if it were a matter of life or death, to figure out what's cool."[2] It should be noted that the repositioning also alienated many loyal advertisers like Paul Marciano, whose striking spreads for Guess had been a fixture in the book since 1982. After pulling his 1991 advertising schedule, Mr. Marciano said, "Because it's Si Newhouse, I gave them the benefit of the doubt. But this is not the sort of magazine I want my ads to appear in. I loved *Details* under Annie Flanders. We didn't fit into their new structure."[3]

PRODUCT IMPROVEMENT

If the introduction of superior competitive products jeopardizes your differential advantage, as we saw with Tenax, you must improve your product quality or risk losing your Alpha brand loyalty. However, if your product is not "broken," do not fix it. For example, when Revlon reformulated and repackaged its Flex shampoo in 1987 in an ill-conceived attempt to update the 20-year-old brand, they alienated much of their existing consumer franchise. Flex's share of the $1.4-billion shampoo market declined from an impressive 5.6 percent in 1986 to 3 percent in 1990, prompting the company to "reintroduce" the original formula in 1991.[4]

LINE EXTENSIONS

Marketers who seek to capitalize on their brand equity with line extensions should recognize the inherent risk: If the new product is a logical extension of the existing brand, it may generate incremental sales and enhance the brand identity; but if the new product radically alters or compromises the brand identity, it will either succeed only at the expense of the core brand, or it will fail and damage the brand identity. Marketers should follow the advise of H. John Greeniaus, president-ceo of Nabisco Brands, who attributes the growth of the company's $450-million Oreo cookie business to line extensions based on "knowing what the brand is, and is not, in consumers' minds."[5] On the other hand, the demise of the wine cooler category was due, in part, to the proliferation of line extensions, which contributed to consumers' flavor-of-the-month perception and lack of product loyalty.

NEW BRANDS

New brands are the lifeblood of many industries, but marketers should resist the temptation to introduce new products that offer no perceived differential advantage. First, they are likely to fail.

According to Phil Lempert, editor of the Lempert Report, more than 12,000 new products were introduced in 1990;[6] estimates of the new product failure rate range from 80 percent (Martin Friedman, editor of Gorman's New Product News)[7] to 95 percent (Mr. Greeniaus of Nabisco Brands).[8] Second, new product introductions are extremely costly; it is almost impossible to introduce a new brand today for less than $10 million, and costs can easily rise to $50 or $60 million. Third, the proliferation of new products can diminish the consumers' perception of value; as Arie L. Kopelman, president of Chanel, noted, "The fragrance industry has cheapened itself in the eyes of the consumer by continual launches. It's lost the hints of exclusivity it once enjoyed."[9]

SUBSIDIARIES

Some companies may find that the establishment of independent subsidiaries or businesses facilitates the creation of a distinctive brand identity, which we have seen is a critical factor in successful Alpha marketing. For example, Wolfgang Puck has opened several different restaurants instead of a Spago chain. And the Estée Lauder Company has set up autonomous divisions for its various cosmetics brands (Estée Lauder, Clinique, Prescriptives, Aramis, Origins Natural Resources), which has enabled them to create distinctive brand identities and effectively segment the market. Many Japanese companies, on the other hand, believe in creating a monolithic corporate identity under the assumption that the company's reputation for quality in one category may be directly transferred to another. Yamaha, for example, manufactures a variety of products, from motorycles to musical instruments—all marketed under the Yamaha name.

ACQUISITIONS

Other companies may want to consider acquisitions that will complement their existing businesses. For example, Perrier Group of America recognized that the Perrier brand did not appeal to all consumers of bottled water and wisely acquired nine other brands, including Poland Spring, Great Bear, and Ozark. Today, the combined brands have a 20 percent share of the U.S. bottled water market.[10] Similarly, the Procter & Gamble Company acquired the upscale Vidal Sassoon and Pantene haircare brands to complement their existing mass market brands, like Head & Shoulders and Pert Plus.

Acquisitions that represent an entirely different industry, such as Sony's recent purchases of CBS records and Columbia Pictures for $5.6 billion, are more problematic and frequently require a long-term perspective. Sony, for example, clearly realizes that this new entertainment property acquisition strategy will take years to pay off. But the company recognized that world demand for audio and video products is projected to grow only 4 percent a year through the end of the century, according to Jardine Fleming Securities in Tokyo, whereas software, such as music and films, will continue growing 17 percent a year or more.[11] In the face of growing competition in the consumer electronics industry, Sony will have a distinct advantage with the unique ability to influence global trends in electronics and entertainment. As Michael Schulhof, president of Sony USA, explains, "unless you have software to support your hardware, you can't have a successful industry."[12] It remains to be seen how successful Sony will be in the free-wheeling entertainment industry. Sony will have to resist the temptation to interfere in businesses that it does not fully understand, as Avon's nearly fatal mismanagement of Tiffany & Company or the General Mills experience with Izod Lacoste demonstrated.

JOINT VENTURES

Joint ventures may enable you to capitalize on the equity and managerial expertise of another business without the risk and financial exposure of an acquistion. For example, the Eureka restaurant cum pub beer factory in Los Angeles is an $8.5-million venture between the Eureka Brewing Company and celebrity chef Wolfgang Puck.[13] The magic culinary touch of Mr. Puck provides the Eureka Brewing Company with an aura that management hopes will enable it to expand distribution and increase production from 12,000 barrels a year to 50,000 barrels, while their substantial financial investment enabled Mr. Puck to create a distinctive new restaurant.

LICENSING

As with the introduction of line extensions, marketers must carefully consider the impact the licensed product will have on their core business. If it will enhance the brand and generate incremental revenue, licensing can be a valid approach. According to *The Licensing Letter*, an industry publication, $66.6-billion worth of licensed goods were sold at retail in 1990, nearly a fivefold increase over the $13.6 billion sold in 1981. Apparel represented nearly one-fourth of all licensed merchandise sold in 1990; the other leading product categories were toys/games, furnishings, gifts, publishing, food/beverage, electronics, health/beauty, and sporting goods.[14] Licensees typically pay royalties of 5 to 10 percent of a product line's wholesale cost according to Murray Altchuler, the executive director of the International Licensing Industry Merchandisers Association.[15] The Disney Company's licensing program, for example, keeps their entertainment properties highly visible and represents a $1.5-billion business.[16] However, marketers should avoid licensing arrangements with companies who will not maintain their standards of quality. They should also recognize the risk of image-destructive licensing. For example, when Halston started "designing" clothes for J.C. Penney, he sacrificed his exclusive image, and sales of his upscale products, from apparel to fragrance, never recovered.

Whatever your rationale and strategy for targeting Alpha consumers, remember that a long-term perspective is usually required. Due to their limited numbers, Alpha consumers alone are unlikely to generate immediate sales increases. However, their endorsement over time may be the key to establishing—and maintaining—a desirable identity for your business.

CHAPTER 13

SEMIOTICS

Semiotics, the analysis and meaning of signs and symbols, play a critical role in targeting Alpha consumers, who tend to be more conscious than the mainstream of signs and symbols. Everything a company does sends a distinct message to consumers; the summation of these messages equals the company's identity in their minds. All identity ultimately comes from inside the company. It cannot be artificially created, because Alpha consumers will always be able to detect inconsistencies in a company's identity, however subtle they may be. This is why self-examination should be an integral part of your strategic planning process (see p. 103–106). As we have seen, the establishment of a desirable corporate or brand identity that enables the Alpha consumer to develop an emotional bond with a product or service is second in importance only to perceived quality in building brand loyalty. Some of the semiotics involved in Alpha marketing follow.

THE COMPANY

This includes its heritage, ownership, location, offices, stationery, personnel, and management policies. The following are a few examples of corporate semiotics that sent clear messages to Alpha consumers.

Bergdorf Goodman and Nordstrom discontinued successful businesses that were no longer compatible with their corporate philosophies. When Halston licensed his name to J.C. Penney, Bergdorf Goodman immediately stopped selling his upscale merchandise. When the animal rights movement crystallized and fur coats became a symbol of the conspicuous consumption of the 1980s, Nordstrom closed its fur salons. These symbolic actions enhanced the Alpha consumer's esteem for those companies.

When Walt Disney Studios announced in 1991 that they would no longer book their movies into theaters that screened commercials preceding the feature (something the Alpha consumer resented), they enhanced their corporate integrity and restored the appeal of going to the movies.

When Jay Chiat selected Frank Gehry, a visionary and controversial architect, to design Chiat/Day/Mojo's new corporate headquarters in Los Angeles, he reinforced the agency's reputation for visionary and controversial advertising.

In 1990 when Hearst Magazines hired Gael Love (former editor of *Fame*, the defunct celebrity magazine, and former associate publisher of *Interview*) to replace Thomas Hoving (former director of the Metropolitan Museum) as editor-in-chief of *Connoisseur* magazine, the company sent a clear signal to readers, and advertisers, that there were going to be significant changes in the product. (Hearst president D. Claeys Bahrenburg said, "I've clearly given her the mandate that I want the circulation grown ... I would say it is her intent to popularize the magazine").[1]

Businesses that do not work "on spec" suggest a greater level of self-worth than businesses that frantically undertake speculative assignments, like the advertising agencies that pitch every account they can, regardless of compatibility.

MARKETING

This includes product quality, name, positioning, pricing, distribution, merchandising, customer service, promotion, advertising, and public relations. Following are a few examples of marketing semiotics that you should consider before you plan your strategy.

• Alpha consumers will buy a product at a premium price, because they perceive it to be of high quality, or at a very low price, because they perceive all the products in the same category to be the same. For example, when purchasing that critical pair of sunglasses, some people in Los Angeles will pay $200 for a pair of designer frames at L.A. Eyeworks on Melrose, while others will buy the knockoffs at the stands on the Venice boardwalk for $5. As Rance Crain of *Advertising Age* points out, "Where you don't want to get caught is in the middle, because people will think that your product isn't the highest quality or the cheapest."[2]

• Advertising diminishes your exclusivity. It announces to the Alpha consumer that your product is for everyone. In discussing the club scene in Manhattan, Michael Musto of the *Village Voice* noted, "Advertising turns a lot of people off (which is why most clubs don't advertise). It demystifies a place and makes it a little less special because it means that they are trying to pull in basically anyone who is willing to pay. They lose a touch of class by doing that." Eric Petterson, owner of Coffee Shop and Live Bait, two ultrahip restaurants in Manhattan frequented by many models, stylists, and photographers, adds, "If you start to advertise, people assume you must be herding."[3]

• Promotional premiums devalue your product. They send the signal to the Alpha consumer that you must bribe people to patronize your business. In the women's prestige fragrance business, for example, where premiums have become institutionalized, unit sales have declined 30 percent in the last 10 years because the product has lost much of its perceived value.

• Product downsizing, decreasing package size while maintaining the same price, is likely to be noticed by savvy Alpha consumers who regard it as a deceptive price increase that raises questions about the integrity of the manufacturer. ("It's a price increase any way you slice it," admits Scott Stewart, a spokesperson for Procter & Gamble Company's diaper division, which recently reduced the number of diapers in a package of Pampers from 88 to 80 while retaining the same price, effectively a 9.1 percent price increase.[4])

• Metal detectors at the entrance to your establishment—at the Sound Factory night club in New York, for example—add an undeniable sense of danger and excitement to the consumer's experience.

• Sometimes what you *do not* do is as important as your marketing program. For example, the total absence of television and telephones was part of the initial appeal of Club Med for Alpha consumers, a tangible symbol of the escape a trip to Club Med represented.

• Under the management of Geraldine Stutz, Henri Bendel did not carry women's clothing above a size 8, and during the Walter Hoving era at Tiffany, the store did not carry diamond rings for men. Each marketer was willing to sacrifice potential sales to protect his exclusive image; they sent a very clear message to consumers that certain types of people were not welcome in their stores.

• At John's Pizzeria, an institution among hip consumers in Greenwich Village, the refusal to sell pizza by the slice reinforces its stature as a "real" restaurant and discourages the hoi polloi from invading.

• Businesses without signage or street identification, such as the Romeo Gigli Boutique on East 69th Street in New York or the Olive Restaurant on Fairfax Avenue in Los Angeles (whose regulars include Madonna, Malcolm McLaren, and David Bowie), similarly discourage walk-in business and protect their insider's cachet.

Clearly, there are no rules. Every business must determine what message it wants to send to Alpha consumers and be cognizant of the semiotics involved.

SPAZIO ROMEO GIGLI IN NEW YORK
The highly original Italian designer's boutique on East 69th street. The lack of street identification contributes to its exclusivity.

CHAPTER 14

VISUAL DESIGN

We have seen how the frequent Alpha involvement—whether by profession or avocation—in highly visual fields, from art and graphic design to fashion and film, enhances Alphas' appreciation of visual style and energy. We have also seen how their visual sensibility has been shaped by their foreign travels to countries like France and Italy where they have been exposed to esthetics that are quite different from the United States. Finally, we have seen how distinctive visual design contributes to the Alpha perception of uniqueness or product differentiation, which is a major factor in purchase motivation, whether it involves fashion (e.g., Chanel), merchandising (e.g., The Body Shop), packaged goods (e.g., Perrier), electronics (e.g., Sony), cars (e.g., Mazda Miata), hotels (e.g., the Morgan Hotel Group), or entertainment (e.g., MTV). Although every design project must be approached independently, in this chapter we identify issues that marketers should consider and generate some guidelines.

PROCEDURES

Always start with a clean slate. Try to discard any preconceptions you may have, because they may stifle creativity. The development of the Swatch watch, for example, represented a virtual negation of all the industry's traditional concepts. Look beyond your immediate product category or business for inspiration; you may discover a new approach in a totally unrelated field that will enable you to preempt the competition. For example, Nike's engagement of a trained architect, Tinker Hatfield, to design its athletic shoes enabled the company to transform the humble sneaker into a high-tech product that commanded high-tech prices. At Kohler, a privately held company in Kohler, Wisconsin, which manufactures toilets, bathtubs, and sinks, artists are recruited from around the country to work in the factory for a four-month period with the goal of rethinking art and bathroom fixtures.

Do not copy your competitors. Alpha consumers' respect for originality and authenticity will work against you, as we observed in their brand loyalty to Levi jeans and resistance to perceived imitations. And if you do copy your competitors, make certain that all of the nuances are correct. Burt Simm Avedon, president of Willis & Geiger, the one-time outfitter to sportsmen like Cornelius Vanderbilt and Ernest Hemingway, attributes the longevity of his firm to its authenticity: "People who try to knock us off don't always understand us."[1]

Do not permit the quest for novelty to undermine your purpose; visual design must be appropriate for the category and compatible with your identity. For example, if you manufacture state-of-the-art electronics, like Sony or Bang and Olufson, design should be sleek and modern and decidedly high-tech. But if you are in the packaged food industry, design should be the exact opposite: rounded shapes, nonplastic materials, and traditional graphics to suggest natural ingredients and homemade freshness, as in the Perrier bottle or Grey Poupon mustard jar.

Invest in visual design, because it will usually provide a significant payback; if you cut corners in an attempt to reduce costs, you send the distinct message to the consumer that you do not care. The investment may involve new personnel, like Karl Lagerfeld at Chanel or Robert Hall at Mazda, or commissioned designs from artists with an established Alpha following, like postmodern architect Michael Graves's work in glass for Steuben or performance artist Peter Schroff's creations for Gotcha sportswear. The investment may require custom molding (instead of stock componentry) and top-grade materials. For example, at the new Paramount hotel in New York designed by Philippe Starck, even the toothbrushes were custom molded, making a distinct design statement about the hotel. (Like the furniture that Mr. Starck designed for The Royalton hotel, the Paramount

ARCHAIC VESSELS BY MICHAEL GRAVES FOR STEUBEN
The post modern architect with an Alpha following was commissioned
by Steuben to work in glass.

toothbrushes are now sold at retail, generating incremental sales and invaluable publicity for the hotel.) Finally, the investment may involve interior design, such as Peter Marino's stylish work for the Barneys New York and Emporio Armani stores or Sam Lopata's whimsical interiors for the Lox Around the Clock, Vince & Eddie's, and Pig Heaven restaurants in New York.

Make visual design an integral part of your marketing strategy. If you want to update or reposition an existing product or service, for example, changes in design should represent a logical evolution of your heritage, as we saw at Chanel and The Gap. If you are introducing a new line, recognize that it must have a core design identity or visual signature if you want to develop a classic brand that will have a long product life cycle. This is one of the differences between long-term successes, like Levi jeans or Harley-Davidson motorcycles, and short-term successes with a flavor-of-the-month perception, like Swatch watch.

MNEMONICS

Mnemonics, visual cues that trigger the consumer's memory, can play an important part in keeping your product top of mind. They may involve your brand name and visual identity. For example, by adopting a fruit as its symbol, Apple Computer Company was able to break through the technical visual imagery that dominated the computer industry and suggest that its products are user-friendly. Similarly, the adoption of polo as its symbol provided the Ralph Lauren business with an immediate upscale identity in the image-driven fashion industry in a way that the name Ralph Lauren or Ralph Lipschitz (Mr. Lauren's real name) could not. A distinctive logo may also play an important role. Every time consumers see the red Levi pocket tab on a pair of jeans or the interlocking Coco Chanel "C's" or the Harley-Davidson eagle, they are reminded of the manufacturer (even when the merchandise is clearly counterfeit). Distinguishing shapes (e.g., the Absolut vodka bottle), materials (e.g., the green glass used in the Perrier bottles), and graphics (e.g., the red and white triangular design on the Marlboro cigarette package) can function in a similar way.

LOX AROUND THE CLOCK IN NEW YORK
Designed by Sam Lopata, the bold exterior alerts the Alpha consumer to the restaurant's hip sensibility where they relate well to its off-beat interior.

The ultimate measure of a successful mnemonic: the con-fiscation of a company's logo or design by young urban blacks for line extensions never envisioned by the original manufacturer, such as Chanel baseball caps, Nike bicycles, and Porsche back-packs.

PRODUCT AND PACKAGE DESIGN

Design can fulfill certain spiritual needs, which is why we are increasingly seeing the Bauhaus esthetic (streamlined, machine-styled) giving way to ergonomics (the symbiosis of design and the human form). Many Alpha consumers in the 1990s are seek-ing comforting, anthropomorphic, user-friendly products that re-flect their usage, whether it is the Gillette Sensor razor, the Canon Photura camera or the oversized chairs and sofas stuffed with down at the Shabby Chic stores in Santa Monica and Soho. Carl Levine, Bloomingdale's senior vice president for furniture and rugs, noted that consumers today "want something that's easy to relate to . . . soft-looking . . . not challenging."[2]

The choice of materials also influences the consumer's per-ception of your product. Examples include:

- Metal. Suggests precision and durability; it is one of the reasons an Alpha consumer might choose a Krups Cap-pucino Maker over a plastic Mr. Coffee machine.

- Glass. Suggests elegance and classicism; it is one of the reasons an Alpha consumer might choose Clarins skincare over another botanical line that was packaged in plastic.

- Plastic. Suggests disposability and artificiality; it is one of the reasons an Alpha consumer might choose Grey Poupon mustard in a glass jar over French's Dijon mustard in a plastic container.

- Paper. Suggests freshness and environmentalism; it is one of the reasons that an Alpha consumer might choose freshly ground coffee in a paper bag over Maxwell House coffee in a can.

Do not overpackage your product; most Alpha consumers

will object to the unnecessary expense, the environmental implications, and your attempt to misrepresent your product. Flagrant examples include most compact disks and roll-on deodorants (which come in virtual chipboard temples). Successful examples of packaging reduction range from the elimination of secondary packaging at The Body Shop to the elimination of tags and strings on the Celestial Seasonings herbal tea bags.

Color and graphics are critical. Try to look beyond your competitors for new directions; try to disregard your preconceptions. Why must computers be beige? Why not consider a palette that reflects trends in fashion or interior design? Why must tissue boxes feature kitschy graphic designs? Why not consider a classic William Morris print or commission a design from a contemporary artist? Look at the European approach to design in your category. If you are in the chocolate candy bar category, look at a Lindt product from Switzerland with its foil innerwrap and luscious four-color photograph of the ingredients on the glossy paper sleeve instead of a Snickers bar in its brown sealed wrapper. If you are in the feminine hygiene category, look at the chic Confetti package from Kimberly Clark in Europe with its colorful graphics (reminiscent of cosmetics or lingerie) instead of the dull gray Kotex box (reminiscent of the school nurse).

ENVIRONMENTAL DESIGN

The environment in which the Alpha consumer encounters your business has a significant impact on his or her purchase behavior. This includes everything from merchandising and visual display to architecture and interior design. Some environments transport the consumer to a different frame of mind that stimulates purchase; the consumer wants to spend time there. The environment may be a retail store, a restaurant, a hair salon, or a bank. It may be upscale (e.g., Bergdorf Goodman, Georgette Klinger) or downscale (e.g., The Gap, The Living Room Coffee House on La Brea Boulevard in Los Angeles), understated (e.g., Barneys New York, The Four Seasons Restaurant in New York) or funky (e.g., the Chateau Marmont Hotel on Sunset Boulevard in Los Angeles, Marion's Continental Restaurant and Lounge on the Bowery in New York), but it should reflect a level of taste and sophistication that the Alpha consumer can relate to. In his avant-garde clothing store in New York, bbc, owner Chris Brick says that he is striving for "that mixed media effect that entertains someone into buying. Basically Dean & Deluca—a stylish food emporium in Soho—has proven that it's possible to sell potatoes in a boutique. They're very expensive potatoes, but they're surrounded by lots of other interesting things."[3]

In a perfect world, marketers would control their business environments with their own distribution channels, as we have seen with the Morgan Hotel Group or The Body Shop. Unfortunately, we do not live in a perfect world, and most marketers must distribute their products in environments over which they have limited control. However, there are steps a marketer can take to present a product to its best advantage:

- Create a uniform visual identity so that the consumer will instantly recognize your product regardless of the environment. On a large scale, this may involve the establishment of in-store boutiques à la Chanel; on a smaller scale, marketers may be limited to signage and display. But the merchandising should be consistent.

- Work with the visual display departments of your distribution channels to maximize your presence. Take advantage of merchandising opportunities, from endcases and outposts to windows and vitrines.

- Do not allow your product to be chained or locked up; this challenges the consumer to buy it—and most often she or he will not bother. Michael Waldock, president of The Body Shop in the United States, attributes much of the company's success in this country to the store's well-stocked, open shelves, which contrast sharply to the ambience in department stores where consumers are separated from the merchandise by a counter. "People come in and just play," says Mr. Waldock.[4]

- If you are repackaging your product, the transition should be accomplished in a clean sweep. Be willing to take back obsolete inventory because a mixture of old and new packaging on display is confusing and visually unappealing.

- Finally, make visual merchandising a priority for your salespeople. Inventory should be well-stocked and maintained in an orderly fashion. Merchandise with that picked-over look is a deterrent to purchase.

As with the other elements involved in targeting the Alpha consumer, an attention to detail in all aspects of visual design will be noticed and appreciated and predispose this discerning consumer to patronizing your business.

CHAPTER 15

DISTRIBUTION AND LOCATION

The Alpha consumer's perception of your business is influenced by the surroundings in which you conduct it—in other words, the company-that-you-keep. For example, if this consumer only encounters your product in upscale specialty stores, like Saks Fifth Avenue and Neiman Marcus, she or he will feel differently about it than if it is available in broad-based department stores, like The Broadway or Hudson's. If your restaurant is located in an offbeat neighborhood, this consumer will feel differently about it than if it is in an established area. In planning your distribution or location strategy, you must first analyze the Alpha consumer's purchase motivation in your category or industry. For example, when purchasing commodities, like household products or toiletries, or selecting a basic service, like a checking account or a dry cleaner, convenience is key; this busy consumer does not want to travel for these goods and services. On the other hand, when selecting specialty goods, like apparel or furniture, or services, like restaurants or hair salons, image becomes much more important; a special trip is sometimes part of the experience and contributes to the perception of product differentiation. Once you have identified the Alpha consumer's purchase motivation, you must decide what marketing statement you want to make and plan your distribution or location strategy accordingly. In this chapter, we examine distribution and location philosophies separately because the issues involved are different for sole proprietors and for manufacturers who distribute their products in channels they do not control.

DISTRIBUTION

If you are marketing an established product or service, carefully evaluate your existing channels of distribution to ascertain whether they are compatible with your brand identity. Be willing to close marginal distribution channels with limited profitability; the damage to your image and long-term growth potential is seldom worth it. We have seen how Chanel and Nike successfully protected their images by pulling out of stores that did not enhance their brand identities. If you are expanding distribution, proceed with caution. We have seen how Izod Lacoste and Trivial Pursuit alienated their existing customer franchises when they went into discount stores; their original customers felt betrayed because they did not see themselves as discount store shoppers. Moreover, scarcity sometimes makes a product more desirable. Harley-Davidson, for example, deliberately limits production and distribution of its "Hogs": "Enough motorcycles is too many motorcycles," according to James H. Paterson, head of the motorcycle division.[1]

If you are introducing a new product, you have many options. In general, if you limit the initial distribution and gradually expand it, you are more likely to achieve long-term success. There are several reasons for this. First, you will encourage the Alpha consumer to become your exclusive customer. This will generate the critical consumer buzz and create the insider's cachet that was characteristic of many of the Alpha marketing successes we studied, from American Express to Perrier. It will also instill in the Alpha consumer a sense of ownership, which is likely to translate into brand loyalty; when the mainstream discovers your brand and you expand distribution, you will not alienate the Alpha consumer because he or she will still consider the brand "his" or "hers." The brand loyalty of the Alpha consumer will enable you to maintain a desirable brand identity over time in the eyes of the mainstream, which usually translates into market share, economies of scale, and impressive profit margins.

Grey Poupon mustard is a textbook example. When the product was introduced in the United States 20 years ago, it was sold in gourmet food stores; and advertising was limited to upscale magazines. This gave the Alpha consumer time to exclusively "own" the brand. When the mainstream discovered nouvelle cuisine and Dijon mustard in the early 1980s, the company significantly expanded supermarket distribution and invested in heavy television advertising. Andrew Langer, who had been president of the Marschalk advertising agency that had the account, discussed the challenge Grey Poupon faced at the time: "If we were going to grow, we couldn't remain in the low-volume gourmet section. . . . But we also didn't want to drive away the gourmets when they realized that Grey Poupon was in their neighbor's fridge. We were on a tightrope: Could we talk to the rest of the world and not lose those people?"[2] Today, Grey Poupon is served at Wendy's and ranks second in dollar sales in this country only to the R. T. French Company,[3] but Alpha consumers do not mind because they still consider the brand "theirs."

There are also strong trade arguments in support of a highly controlled distribution strategy. As with Alpha consumers, retailers or distributors are more likely to aggressively support your business if they experience a sense of ownership; this is difficult to accomplish if all of their competitors also sell your product. The spectacular failure of the upscale Christian Lacroix fragrance for women, which was introduced with considerable fanfare in 600 stores in 1990 by the Louis Vuitton Moet Hennessey conglomerate, was largely due to the lack of exclusivity. Cosmetics industry consultant Allan Mottus noted, "Because of its broad distribution, no one was made to feel special."[4] Moreover, if you create the perception of success in select distribution channels, you will build trade demand for your product and maximize your leverage with other retailers or distributors when you are ready to expand.

If you plan to pursue a controlled distribution strategy, always start at the top. It is relatively easy to expand distribution from upscale to downscale channels—and almost impossible to go in the opposite direction. Be willing to sacrifice short-term volume for long-term growth. Once you go into mass volume retailers, there is no turning back. Explore image-building channels where you are likely to gain the endorsement of professionals or aficionados. If you are introducing a new beer, for example, consider limiting initial distribution to hip bars and restaurants; consumers often like to try new beers when they go out. They will then attempt to purchase your product in retail stores, and the chagrined retailers will beg you to sell them your new beer. However, you must expand distribution quickly enough that you do not permit competitors to move in ahead of you.

Finally, consider establishing your own distribution channels. This represents the wave of the future as Alpha consumers increasingly reject general merchandise stores and supermarkets in favor of highly focused specialty stores. We have seen the advantages of having your own stores in our discussion of The Gap and The Body Shop. Chanel and Nike are opening more of their own stores, and others are likely to follow their lead. The benefits of establishing your own distribution channels are multiple. First, it enables you to assume complete control of your business, from merchandising to service personnel; you have the opportunity to create a total environment that reinforces your identity and stimulates purchase. It also helps you to keep in direct touch with your consumer, so that you can respond more quickly to shifts in market demand. It provides you with an expedient, and very private, arena for test marketing, and the elimination of middlemen permits you to get new products into market that much faster. And perhaps most important, the vertical integration of your business generally leads to greater profitability. If you do not have the complete product line to justify your own outlet, explore the possibility of joint ventures with complementary manufacturers. For example, fragrance manufacturers who object to the rising cost of conducting business in department stores (at the same time that store traffic is declining) might investigate the specialized European parfumerie approach; it is infinitely more appealing to consumers and likely to be more profitable.

LOCATION

If you are fortunate enough to control the distribution of your product or service, the location that you select for your business should be consistent with your identity and, at the same time, compatible with the Alpha consumer's purchase behavior. We have seen that Alpha consumers increasingly choose to patronize neighborhood businesses. Convenience, of course, is a factor, but more important is the desire to escape the anonymity of life in urban America, which can be alienating at times. Many Alpha consumers long to experience the sense of community that they have observed in European cities, where people often develop personal relationships with people who work in the local neighborhood business establishments and share common concerns. This bonding with the Alpha consumer in the neighborhood will help to ensure the longevity of your business. Gael Greene, restaurant critic for *New York* magazine, explains, "If you don't have something to give the neighborhood when the heat cools, you've had it."[5]

There is also a strong economic argument to support the location of your business in a transitional area where Alphas are likely to live: The cost of real estate or rental space is usually relatively low. This will enable you to keep your operational expenses low enough that you can afford to pass the savings on to your customers while protecting your profit margins at the same time. (The 1980s are over, and consumers are increasingly value-conscious; the downscaling in restaurant pricing that we have observed in the last few years is one salient example.) At the same time, your investment in real estate or a long-term lease is likely to appreciate: Once Alpha consumers start moving into an area, it invariably becomes fashionable, and the value of the real estate increases. Moreover, your identification with the area will enhance your image as a trendsetting business.

The transformation of a marginal area into a desirable one often begins with artists and photographers in search of inexpensive studio space; they frequently gravitate to older industrial buildings and warehouses with large windows and high ceilings. At the same time, nightclub owners are attracted to the cavernous, subterranean spaces of these relatively remote buildings, which enhance their "underground" stature—a critical element in a successful club. Soon art galleries and bohemian restaurants and bars start appearing on the street floors, followed by bookstores and one-of-a-kind boutiques. When the area begins to attract chain stores, movie theaters, and expensive restaurants, the gentrification process will be complete. Abbot Kinney Boulevard (formerly Washington Boulevard) in Los Angeles is a cur-

JAVA BEANS COFFEEHOUSE
This establishment helped to transform Abbot Kinney Boulevard in Los
Angeles from a questionable address to a chic one.

rent example in progress. Ten years ago, the street (which runs
from Santa Monica to LAX) was an artists' domain, complete
with a suitably proletarian dive, "Babe" Brandelli's Brig. Architects, galleries, antique dealers, and boutiques followed. Today,
restaurants are moving in at each end—from Rockenwagner,
¡Sabroso!, A Votre Sante, and the Sculpture Gardens to Hal's,
Capri, and the Java Beans Coffee House—and Abbot Kinney
Boulevard is rapidly becoming a Westside destination.[6]

Although college students often have limited disposable income, they are frequently adventurous and experimental consumers, so businesses with accessible price-points may also want
to consider locations near universities. Moreover, the endorsement of young consumers often contributes to the creation of a
hip brand identity, as we have seen with Nike, Ben & Jerry's,
and The Body Shop.

As with the other elements of your marketing strategy, distribution and location should be consistent with your identity
so that you do not send the consumer conflicting messages.

CHAPTER 16

CUSTOMER SERVICE

As with the environment in which you conduct your business, the service that you provide your customers plays a key role in creating an ambience that motivates purchase. Sometimes customer service is the critical success factor. For example, the Seattle-based Nordstrom specialty apparel stores (1990 sales: about $2.7 billion)[1] have entered new regions and consistently stolen market share from competitors with comparable merchandise and pricing by offering superior customer service. On the other hand, the lack of customer service in Bloomingdale's (1990 sales: about $1.2 billion)[2] has contributed significantly to its downfall. (Bloomingdale's has recently closed four branch stores and is presently under bankruptcy protection.) As the late empress of fashion, Diana Vreeland, proclaimed several years ago with characteristic prescience, "Bloomingdale's is the end of shopping because there isn't anyone to wait on you; you just sort of admire things. Then you see a man; you think he's a floorwalker: 'I'm sorry, lady, I can't help you. I'm like you, I'm just looking for somebody to help me.' So you go out into the street with tears in your eyes: You've accomplished nothing and you've lost your health!"[3] (Mrs. Vreeland's disenchantment with department stores was shared by many: According to the Roper organization, the percentage of adults shopping at a department store once a month declined from 63 percent in 1974 to 51 percent in 1989.[4])

GENERAL GUIDELINES

In planning your customer service program, recognize that it makes a very distinct statement about your business; it should be consistent with your identity. For example, your employees represent your business and should project an image that is consistent with your product or service. Michael Solomon, a consumer psychologist who has done extensive work on the role of appearance in impression management says that groups need "markers of membership" to give them identity and cohesion.[5] Your customer service personnel provide you with a unique opportunity to demonstrate to the Alpha consumer that you share her or his values. David Teiger, CEO of United Research, a management consulting firm, adds, "Everything matters—who you hire, what they say, how they say it, what they look like."[6]

Look beyond your immediate industry or competitors for new direction. For example, Thomas Hoving, former director of the Metropolitan Museum in New York, looked to the travel industry: "When we built a new wing for the museum, we spent a lot of time in airline terminals to study how to move crowds of people around. The first thing you see when you walk into the Met is not art but happy, smiling faces behind a brass information counter. We learned that from Disneyworld: they are masters in hospitality, in making people feel glad they came. Anyone in the museum world who hasn't spent time at Disneyworld is making a big mistake."[7]

Recognize the business potential that each customer represents. If every satisfied customer brings in one additional customer and that customer brings in one additional customer . . . you will soon have a consumer franchise built on positive word-of-mouth, the most desirable foundation for any business. (Conversely, the impact of a negative review from one dissatisfied Alpha customer may ultimately discourage many potential customers from even investigating your business.) Conduct frequent surveys of customer satisfaction. Maintain active preferred customer lists including product preferences and purchase history. If your product or service is widely distributed—such as cars, electronics, apparel, cosmetics, or financial services—consider investing in a satellite data network that would provide instant transmission of the customer's history to each of your sales outlets. Try to develop a personal relationship with your customers; keep them informed of new products and special offers. Provide substantial incentives for salespeople, dealers, and distributors who maintain high levels of customer satisfaction. Richard Melman, founder and president of Lettuce Entertain You enterprises, a privately held corporation in Chicago that owns and manages 30 restaurants, including Ed Debevic's, a chain of retro diners with annual sales in excess of $100 million, largely attributes its success to special incentives for its waiters and waitresses. "We've always said that if the waiters are happy, the customers will be happy," said Mr. Melman.[8] (According to *Newsweek*, the "unusually strong emphasis on good service does a great deal to convince people they're enjoying themselves . . . even if the food is uninspired."[9])

Exceed customer expectations; provide extras free of charge (simply build the cost into your basic price). Examples include:

- Restaurants that serve their customers a complimentary glass of champagne when guests are seated or truffles with their coffee.
- Hotels with fresh fruit and flowers in every guest room.
- Auto repair dealers who wash, wax, and fill with gasoline the cars that they service.
- Businesses that provide "loaner" products while the customer's is being repaired.
- Movie theaters with gourmet concessions, like espresso and brownies, instead of popcorn and soft drinks.
- Supermarkets with fresh juice bars.

Do not cost control yourself out of business. Recognize that your investment in staffing, training, and employee incentives will generate ample returns. (And a failure to invest in customer service may prove fatal as the demise of the department store attests.)

Encourage trial. For example:

- Apparel stores should have gracious dressing rooms with great mirrors.
- Gourmet food stores should provide "tasting" opportunities wherever feasible.
- Bookstores should have comfortable seating for serious browsers.

- Art galleries and antique dealers should permit prospective buyers to take pieces home on approval.

Facilitate purchase. For example:

- Offer an unconditional satisfaction guarantee and a liberal return policy. This will enhance your integrity and reassure a tentative customer.
- Accept all major credit cards. The Alpha consumer seldom carries cash.
- Encourage phone reservations, appointments, and advance sales. For example, the AMC movie theaters in Los Angeles and the Loews theaters in New York now provide phone-ahead credit card ticket sales. (For a service charge of 75 cents a ticket, you can call for tickets for specific performances up to three days in advance and pick them up at a special window just before the show.)
- Honor reservations. If necessary, require a credit card minimum guarantee, but do not overbook.
- Provide a toll-free 800 number, preferably available 24-hours a day. (See p. 140–142 on telemarketing.)
- Include free alterations.
- Offer free gift wrapping.
- Provide home delivery. For example, busy women always need new pantyhose, so Esmark apparel will send its Givenchy hosiery directly to the customer's home or office, and provide free overnight delivery for orders of 12 pairs or more.[10]
- Consider establishing a bridal registry. With the demise of the department stores, many other businesses from art galleries to sporting goods stores have successfully entered the market. New York's Metropolitan Museum of Art, for example, has found its bridal registry, created in 1980, to be an effective sales tactic. "It's not our main source of income, but it's still a nice piece of change," said Judith Block, manager of the museum's registry.[11]
- Resist the temptation to book tour groups or conven-

tioneers; they are frequently disruptive, and the chances that they will enhance your image are very slight indeed.

- Have private facilities for your VIP clientele. (Celebrities and philanderers will appreciate the discretion it affords.)
- Do not enforce a strict single-sex restroom policy. (Sharing things—secrets, experiences, and controlled substances—is frequently a co-ed activity.)
- Consider a restrictive door policy. In discussing night clubs, Michael Musto admits that "It's kind of de rigueur—even if everybody ultimately gets in—just because it makes everybody feel a little bit special when they do get in."

MUSIC

If you are going to provide live entertainment or background music, it should be consistent with your identity. For example, the background music in three different New York fashion boutiques reflects the sensibility of the individual designers represented: At Chanel, there is none; at Valentino, it is European rock; and at Ralph Lauren, it is 1930s jazz.

Alpha consumers have diverse musical tastes, so it is impossible to please everyone. As a general rule, your choice of music should either be "classic," whether it is Chopin or Judy Garland, or so arcane that few people will recognize it, whether it is reggae or Les Négresses Vertes; middle-of-the-road pop music should usually be avoided, whether it is Muzak or a Top 40 format. The Alpha consumer's individual preferences are incidental; he or she will respect your conviction.

PERSONNEL

The type of people that you hire should reflect both the nature of your business and the Alpha consumer's purchase motivation. For example, if you are involved in financial services, transportation, or electronics, your personnel should convey a sense of expertise and dependability. A hip image is not only unnecessary, it may actually be detrimental. On the other hand, if you are selling your taste and style—whether you are involved in the fashion, beauty, interior design, hotel, restaurant, florist, or catering industries—your personnel should project your sense of taste and style; image is critical.

At Ian Schrager's new Paramount hotel in Manhattan, personnel was not hired—they were cast by appearance. In a very real sense, they are performers in a theater. Kevin Krier, who was in charge of staffing, admitted that "Experience was not a criterion for employment.... The look of the hotel is young, modern, aware of what's happening in fashion, and we wanted people who would convey that."[12] Mr. Krier received 2,000 applications for 60 positions. In the end, he hired many aspiring actors, models, and writers, along with some fitness trainers from the trendy Soho Training Center. Everyone looks great and contributes to the hotel's distinctive ambience. "Attitude is key," explains Mr. Schrager.[13]

Occasionally, there is a dichotomy between image and competence, particularly when employers hire people with their own agendas who are not committed to the employers' businesses—in other words, the aspiring actors, models, musicians and writers. Although some of these people do become "celebutantes" (Debi Mazar was the doorperson at the Mudd Club) or even bona fide stars (Alec Baldwin was a bartender at Studio 54), marketers should not allow them to coast on their glamour; professionalism is still the bottom line.

The sales approach should be subtle. As we noted, Alpha consumers generally like to obtain the necessary information—and then make their purchase decisions independently. Chris Brick of bbc says of his Alpha clientele, "It has to be soft-sell today. People know how to style themselves—they know what they're looking for."

Finally, personnel should not attempt to become familiar with the customer. For example, they should not address the customers by their first names (or slip them their home phone number). The Alpha consumer wants service, not friendship.

CHAPTER 17

DIRECT MARKETING

As we noted in our discussion of Alpha purchase behavior in chapter 3, the efficacy of direct marketing is declining. Direct mail revenues alone increased from $6.7 billion to $22.1 billion in the last decade, providing evidence of direct marketing saturation.[1] With their myriad magazine subscriptions, memberships, and credit cards, Alpha consumers often seem to be on every direct marketing list available, and they are increasingly taking actionable steps to prevent unsolicited direct marketing appeals, from registering complaints with the Mail Preference Service of the Direct Marketing Association to utilizing new phone services or their telephone answering machines to screen unwanted telemarketing calls. (According to the Direct Marketing Association, more than 1.9 million people have registered for its Mail Preference Service, which will remove a name from 80 percent of the national direct mail advertisers' lists. A similar service, the Telephone Preference Service, reports that 480,000 people have asked to have their names withheld from telemarketing agencies.[2]) A 1990 Harris poll, conducted for consumer-data giant Equifax, showed that 79 percent of respondents were concerned with threats to their personal privacy—up from 47 percent in 1977—further evidence that direct marketers should proceed with caution.[3] Nevertheless, direct marketing can be still be a persuasive approach when you have "news" or information to convey to the Alpha consumer regarding new (or improved) products or services or distribution; it is most effective if you can convey a sense of exclusivity or recognition in your offer, such as a unique product or service not available elsewhere or a private sale for your charge account customers. In 1991, for example, when Bettina Riedel moved her specialty clothing boutique in New York to a larger space on Spring Street in Soho, she decided not to run any ads—and just sent mail pieces to "4,122 customers" instead: The new 3,500-square-foot store generated $30,000 in sales the opening weekend. "We have a really established addict customer," noted Miss Riedel.[4]

DIRECT MAIL

According to the U.S. Postal Service, in 1990 Americans received more than 63 billion pieces of third-class mail—and tossed out an estimated 15 percent of it unopened.[5] To encourage the Alpha consumer to peruse your mail piece or catalog, instead of discarding it immediately with the Publishers Clearing House Sweepstakes, the Victoria's Secret catalog, and the rest of the nightmare mail she or he receives, there are some general guidelines to follow.

Stimulate curiosity with a striking visual design or novel presentation. Do not compromise on creative development or production costs. Too often mail pieces receive too little marketing attention. They are frequently considered a commodity to be produced as cheaply as possible, and it shows. For design direction and new ideas, direct marketers should look to the innovative invitations and catalogs sent by many art galleries, for example, where the invitation can "make or break a show" according to Edith Newhall in *New York* magazine.[6] Not surprisingly, gallery invitations have become collectors' items, so you may want to investigate past as well as current approaches. Or look at European mail pieces. For example, the innovative Next Directory mail order catalog of women's fashions published in London includes fabric swatches and a glossy hard cover. ("We wanted to produce a volume that people would put in their libraries next to the Charles Dickens," said Judy Bracher, public relations manager for Next.[7])

If you want to position yourself as a "classic" business and plan to pursue a long-term direct marketing strategy, you may want to consider a classic presentation that varies only slightly over time. This approach has been successfully employed by companies like Clinique and Tiffany, whose consistency always prompts immediate brand recognition as the consumer sorts his or her mail.

If you are enclosing your mail piece in an envelope, there are several "tricks" to employ that may encourage the Alpha recipient to at least open it. Avoid the obvious symbols of junk mail, like mailing labels or "occupant" addressee. Consider investing in first class stamps; the third-class mail bulk postage meter does not exactly create a sense of exclusivity or urgency. Only include your company name on the envelope if you are confident of your brand equity; otherwise, it is safer to list only your return address and keep the consumer guessing.

Solo or independent mail pieces, where you have total control of the image and distribution, are generally more effective than omnibus mailings, inserts in Sunday newspaper supplements, or store-initiated catalogs. Chanel, for example, always creates its own mail pieces (even when the program involves their retail accounts), which is one reason that the brand enjoys such a distinctive identity in the minds of the consumer.

Do not devalue your direct mail offer in the mind of the consumer by frequency; carefully merge-and-purge your mailing lists, so that you do not approach the same consumer more than four times a year. For example, although the J. Crew catalogues of classic understated sportswear are handsomely produced and visually appealing, most Alpha consumers receive them 14 times a year, which has considerably diminished their impact: The annual growth in the J. Crew mail order business has subsequently declined from 25 percent to 30 percent in the early 1980s to less than 15 percent.[8]

The amount of explicit product information that you should include depends on your strategic objective. If you hope to stimulate mail order purchase, you should include a comprehensive product description, an unconditional customer satisfaction guarantee, and an accommodating return policy; this consumer is not likely to gamble on the unknown. If you hope to generate immediate traffic in your establishment, whether it is a store, a restaurant, or a salon, you should include a significant incentive or an innovative offer with a limited period of availability. For example, a restaurant might feature a "guest" chef or a special menu based on seasonal ingredients. Standard "bribes" like discounts, coupons, and premiums are usually insufficient incentives for the Alpha consumers—and likely to tarnish your image in their eyes. If you hope to create awareness or enhance your image, the approach should be decidedly soft sell. For example, in 1990 when the Twentieth Century Fox Film Corporation was promoting the film *Miller's Crossing*, targeted consumers in Manhattan received a slick, four-color, multipage direct mail piece that resembled a playbill with background information on the film and its creators—and a discreet announcement that the film would premiere exclusively at the Coronet Theater on September 22d. And Emporio Armani sends to highly targeted consumers a beautiful, oversized, 100-page international life-style magazine in English and Italian that includes articles, interviews, and arts and entertainment reviews; there are striking photographs of Armani-clad models but no product information beyond the location of the Emporio Armani boutiques throughout the world. Of course, this approach is extremely expensive and unlikely to generate an immediate return on your promotional investment. However, the positive word-of-mouth it creates can contribute substantially to your long-term brand equity.

Finally, if you are currently distributing your product exclusively through retail distribution channels, investigate direct marketing opportunities. If you market a product with a high rate of consumption, from household products to pantyhose, consider selling "subscriptions." As with a magazine subscription, the consumer would receive your product on a regular basis. This approach would encourage brand loyalty and maximize profitability at the same time. (With the elimination of the retailer, you should be able to easily absorb the incremental cost of home delivery and still increase your profit margin.)

TELEMARKETING

Although Alpha consumers appreciate toll-free numbers and the convenience of ordering by phone (e.g., The Body Shop does 15 percent of its business by phone order[9]), they resent unsolicited telemarketing calls that they regard as an invasion of privacy.

Not only will these consumers reject your immediate offer, but unsolicited calls also may generate such ill will that Alphas will effectively boycott your business in the future. And many Alpha consumers already have a negative predisposition to telemarketing which they associate with the Home Shopping Network and other television offers, like record collections, Pearl Cream, and "the amazing ginsu knives" that are "not available in any store." (It should be noted that Alpha consumers are not alone in their aversion to telemarketing: According to a 1991 survey by New York advertising agency Warwick Baker & Fiore and *Adweek's Marketing Week*, 75 percent of Americans consider phone advertising an intrusion on privacy and 72 percent find it distasteful.[10])

On the other hand, the availability of a toll-free 800 number is rapidly becoming an essential part of customer service. Over the past decade, the number of toll-free calls on AT&T's 800-line network has grown from 1.3 billion to 8 billion.[11] If you plan to offer telemarketing services, there are a few guidelines to note:

- Include a toll-free 800 number that is operative 24 hours a day; business hours partially defeat the purpose.
- Avoid 900 numbers. Most consumers associate them with phone-sex lines and other sleazy operations; moreover, they resent the additional charge.
- Provide adequate staffing. Phone lines that are perpetually busy generate ill will and discourage many Alpha consumers (who tend to be rather impatient).
- If you are going to play background music while the customer is waiting, note our recommendation regarding music (p. 135).
- Phone operators should be courteous and informed—and proficient in the English language. No customer should receive the impression that he or she has dialed a foreign country by mistake; this does not exactly instill a sense of consumer confidence (unless, of course, you are calling an ethnic restaurant in which case it does lend a certain air of authenticity). At the GE Answer Center, for example, the requirements for the 150 phone representatives now include a college degree and sales experience. Says N.

Powell Taylor, general manager of the Answer Center: "Today's consumer is better educated and more sophisticated ... we need people with good interpersonal skills." This investment in well-trained telemarketing personnel has produced positive results for GE: Since the company first installed its 800 number in 1982, calls have escalated from 1,000 to 65,000 a week.[12]

- Avoid specious sales gimmicks that are only likely to alienate this savvy consumer. For example, in 1991, Chiquita Brands introduced an 800 number that offers meritless medical advice: After divulging information to a "nutritionist" regarding their household profile, and food budget, consumers calling the line receive only two possible menu plans, both of which are, not surprisingly, exceedingly high in banana consumption.[13]

As with direct mail, telemarketing should facilitate purchase without invading the consumer's privacy or insulting his or her intelligence.

CHAPTER 18

PUBLIC RELATIONS

"Your customers are your best advertising," says Chris Brick, owner of bbc. Indeed, savvy marketers regard their Alpha customers as de facto press agents for their businesses. Their implicit endorsement is more persuasive, and far less expensive, than advertising. For example, many Alpha consumers are intrigued when they read:

In *The New Yorker* that Karl Lagerfeld drinks Diet Coke

In the *Celebration* cookbook that James Beard drank Glenfiddich

In *Advertising Age* that James Brady drinks Stolichnaya on the rocks with an olive

In the *New York Times* that Liza Minnelli smokes Marlboros

In *Details* that Ed McCabe smokes Marlboro Lights

In *Paper* that Claude Montana patronizes Mea Culpa

In *New York* that Madonna buys her lipstick at M.A.C.

In *Vogue* that Ellen Barkin shops at the Comme Des Garçons boutique in Soho

In *HG* that Helmut Newton stays at the Chateau Marmont on Sunset Boulevard

In *Los Angeles* that Jack Nicholson drives an English Range Rover County SE

In *W* that Meryl Streep drives a Volvo

In *Vanity Fair* that Sandra Bernhard is reading *Will You Please be Quiet, Please?* by Raymond Carver

The public relations challenge: how to discreetly capitalize on your influential customers' endorsement. You may want to consider incentives to assure their continued custom, such as complimentary merchandise or a significant discount—a tactic long employed by fashion designers and restaurant owners. You may want to casually mention their patronage to your contacts in the media; as long as you do not exploit your customers, few will object.

Of course, customers who do not enhance your brand image represent a very different kind of public relations challenge: damage control. Boaz Mazor, who arranges the seating at Oscar de la Renta's fashion shows—a critical public relations task because the audience is as important as the clothes—diplomatically explains why some customers have to suffer the indignity of sitting in the second row: "We have one woman who buys a lot, but she's not a fashion plate. And plus, if she did sit in the front row, she wouldn't know what to say to Evangeline Bruce." Employing a classic maître d's strategy, Mr. Mazor adds, "You tell them the second row is a better view anyway."[1]

It is important to cultivate personal relationships with people in the media whose integrity is respected by Alpha consumers. As we noted, these savvy consumers recognize the tremendous pressure on the media to give advertisers favorable mention, particularly in a period of declining advertising budgets. Helen Gurley Brown, the longtime editor of Hearst Corporation's *Cosmopolitan* magazine, maintains that "We just don't say rotten things about advertisers," but Linda Wells, a former editor at Condé Nast's *Vogue* and the current editor-in-chief of the company's new women's magazine *Allure*, admits, "I've seen magazine articles written based on advertisers' requests—I know, I've done it."[2] So marketers should identify people in the media with perceived integrity and develop relationships with them. For example, if your public relations objective is the creation of a hip, social image for your business, pursue George Wayne from *Paper*, not Aileen Mehle ("Suzy") or Liz Smith.

When you hold a public relations event for the media, try to provide an element of novelty and entertainment that will make it memorable and reinforce your strategic objective. This will stimulate the interest of the media and the Alpha consumer who will be exposed to the publicity it will generate. The novelty might include the venue, such as the party Barneys New York held on the 30-yard line of the empty Cotton Bowl stadium (p. 71). Or the novelty might be in the creative execution, such as fashion designer Todd Oldham's inclusion of Billy Beyond, a drag performer well known on the East Village club circuit, with the professional models in his Spring 1991 women's fashion collection. But it should invigorate the media who, not surprisingly, often become rather jaded.

Like your customers, your employees can be a priceless public relations resource, as Condé Nast recognized when they hired Tina Brown as editor-in-chief of *Vanity Fair*, as Tiffany recognized when they commissioned Paloma Picasso to design jewelry, or as Calvin Klein recognized when he engaged David Lynch to direct his new Obsession fragrance commercials in 1990. Every time Tina Brown, Paloma Picasso, or David Lynch appear in

TODD OLDHAM FASHION SHOW
The inclusion of Billy Beyond, a drag performer, with the professional models, helped to make the presentation memorable and enhanced the young designer's reputation for witty, irreverent fashions.

the media, regardless of the context, *Vanity Fair*, Tiffany, and Calvin Klein, respectively, benefit from their professional association. However, a "token" employee whose primary contribution to the business is his or her name is not likely to impress Alpha consumers with their keen sense of integrity. Giorgio Armani, for example, did not exactly enhance his credibility when he engaged socialite/princess/author/actress/talk show hostess/interior decorator/whatever Lee Radziwell Ross as a public relations consultant.

This chapter briefly explores some aspects of public relations: new business/new product introductions; maintaining top-of-mind awareness; philanthropy; sponsorships; and product placement.

NEW BUSINESS/NEW PRODUCT INTRODUCTIONS

If you are starting a new business or introducing a new product, you should focus on a single strategic issue and create a public relations campaign that reinforces it. Your executional options include: a highly targeted Alpha campaign; a slow build; a media blitz; an international approach. We will look at a few recent examples.

• *Targeted Alpha Campaign.* When the Walt Disney Company released *Green Card* on Christmas Day 1990, the company's marketing executives realized that Alpha consumers were the most likely to be interested in the film's director (the Australian, Peter Weir) or stars (Gerard Depardieu, the French actor, and Andie MacDowell, the star of the cult film *sex, lies and videotape*). Consequently, the film was only released in New York and Los Angeles, where there is the greatest concentration of Alpha consumers. Moreover, Disney Studios chairman Jeffrey Katzenberg personally hosted chic screenings followed by receptions at New York's 21 Club, Hollywood's Morton's Restaurant, and the Los Angeles County Museum of Art. Disney marketing chief Robert Levin said it was an effort to reach the "opinion makers" who would generate the type of buzz the film required to attract a broader audience.[3] The strategy worked: Over the next two months distribution was gradually expanded to 700 screens.

Sometimes you may want to target professional Alphas. When Farberware, Inc. was ready to introduce its new Millennium line of high-priced nonstick stainless-steel cookware in the fall of 1990, it sent out complimentary $70 sauté pans to about 100 well-known chefs and cooking school operators. Among the recipients was Jacques Pepin, who gave a cooking demonstration on the NBC "Today Show" and used the distinctive, blue-lined Millennium pan. Kevin O'Malley, group vice president of Farberware, said the company subsequently had "epicureans jumping on the bandwagon."[4]

• *Slow Build.* Ian Schrager compared the opening of his Paramount hotel in Manhattan in the fall of 1990 to "planning an invasion."[5] The invasion began with the creative talent and collaborators Mr. Schrager recruited—each of them a public relations opportunity. Philippe Starck, the avante-garde French designer, made "the Paramount a playground for design-loving adults."[6] Gary Panter, the artist behind Pee-wee Herman's TV playhouse, designed the daycare center. Dean & Deluca, the trendy gourmet food emporium in Soho, opened a take-out counter and espresso bar off the hotel's lobby. Dot Zero, a hip downtown souvenir shop, opened a branch. Edwin Schlossberg, the multimedia artist (and husband of Caroline Kennedy) designed a computerized information center for guests. Bruce Weber created the print advertising. And Madonna's personal trainer served as a consultant in the design of the hotel's gym. With collaborators like these involved, and his own track record, Mr. Schrager had no difficulty obtaining extensive advance coverage in a variety of publications read by Alpha consumers, including hip, downtown magazines (*Paper, Village Voice*); slick, uptown magazines (*Vanity Fair, W*); design books (*HG, Metropolitan Home*); trade publications (*Women's Wear Daily, Restaurant News*); and newspapers (*Wall Street Journal, New York Post*). The Paramount, in fact, presented such a public relations bonanza that the *New York Times* featured the hotel half a dozen times in different sections of the paper, including business, design, and social columns. To officially consecrate the Paramount, Mr. Schrager persuaded Anna Wintour, the editor-in-chief of *Vogue* to hold a party honoring Karl Lagerfeld, Gianni Versace, and Christian Lacroix in the hotel's highly theatrical lobby. This was the ultimate benediction. *Women's Wear Daily* proclaimed it "the first party of the season," the *New York Times* announced that it "opened the new social season," and the Paramount was a direct hit.

• *Media Blitz.* When Simon & Schuster introduced *Nancy Reagan, the Unauthorized Biography* by Kitty Kelley in the spring of 1991, the company took the opposite approach. Prepublication publicity was tightly controlled to ensure maximum media attention when the book was released. The publisher did not sell prepublication serial rights, for example, a move considered rare for such an exposé, and advance copies were tightly guarded. "Usually, there's a lot of prepublication leaking that goes on that can thwart the most tightly controlled plans," said James Milliot, executive editor of *BP Reports*, a book-publishing newsletter, "but they were very successful here."[7] In a brilliant move, a preview copy was given to political cartoonist Garry Trudeau, who began running a series of "Doonesbury" strips about the book on its publication date. The intense secrecy contributed to the media blitz that followed the release of the book. Editors were seemingly racing to cover the book first; there were simultaneous cover stories in *Time, Newsweek,* and the *New York Times* (a major P.R. coup), as well as less-restrained publications like *People* and the supermarket tabloids. In the magazine cover sweepstakes, Mrs. Reagan swept into first place by a wide margin, leaving Madonna and Elizabeth Taylor biting the dust. (The news even reached Eastern Europe: "The book is already famous in Poland!" exclaimed Witold Orzechowski, the Warsaw-based publisher who eagerly acquired the Polish rights.[8])

• *International Approach.* As the wealthiest consumer market in the world, the United States is usually the ultimate goal for marketers. However, we have seen in our discussion of distribution strategies (p. 125-128), how the imprimatur of Paris or London, for example, can create a heightened sense of product demand among Alpha consumers in this country who have first "discovered" products on their foreign travels. Since many Alpha consumers are favorably disposed to foreign products, an international approach to public relations can be a highly effective way to generate a buzz among Alpha consumers in this country. For example, Chanel introduced its Égoïste fragrance for men in Europe in 1990 where it created a sensation among the media, the trade, and consumers. When the company introduced the product in the United States a year later, there was already a fairly high level of awareness among Alpha consumers. Similarly, Cameron Mackintosh, the British producer of megahit musical plays like *Miss Saigon, The Phantom of the Opera*, and *Les Miserables*, always opens his productions on the West End in London—and then waits a year or two to mount a New York production. By the time, Mr. Mackintosh finally opens on Broadway, anticipation is so high that his productions are nearly impervious to the critics' reviews. For example, when *Miss Saigon* opened in New York in 1991, Mr. Mackintosh had already sold $37 million in advance ticket sales, twice the earlier record set by his *Phantom of the Opera*.

MAINTAINING TOP-OF-MIND AWARENESS

Maintaining top-of-mind awareness without risking overexposure is the public relations challenge facing existing businesses. As Gael Greene, restaurant critic for *New York* magazine, notes, "A hip hypester wants his place to be hot, pleasantly hot . . . not fiercely hot, just hot enough—you know, Billy Norwich—*New York Post* gossip columnist—once-a-week hot, not Billy-every-day hot. Such a fine line."[9] Marketers may want to consciously suppress publicity from time to time to avoid the perception of a fad. For example, in 1989, 150 Wooster was the hippest restaurant in New York with weekly media coverage of its clientele. A year later, 150 Wooster closed. (Miss Greene describes it as "the flashiest, fastest fifteen minutes in history.")[10] 150 Wooster owner Brian McNally, whose estimable track record includes Odeon, Cafe Luxembourg, Canal Bar, and Indochine, attributed the demise of 150 Wooster to the dynamics of the restaurant business in New York: "That's inevitable. It's in the nature of trendiness."[11] But the success of Odeon, which is still popular among Alpha consumers after nearly 20 years, demonstrates that it is possible to maintain top-of-mind awareness with a more discreet public relations profile.

IMAGE MAKE-OVERS

Existing businesses that want to change their image with a focused public relations program should proceed cautiously because Alpha consumers, with their myriad sources of insider's information, will be very sensitive to the perception of hypocrisy. For example, when rumors in the mid-1980s that a well-known American fashion designer had AIDS inspired him to conveniently marry one of his design assistants and embark on a major public relations campaign with his new "beard," his integrity was compromised in the eyes of the Alpha consumer who knew that he had been one of the most notoriously indiscreet homosexuals in New York (and the Fire Island Pines and Key West, where he also had homes). As with a product repositioning, image make-overs should not be too abrupt; they should evolve in a logical manner—and not insult the consumer's intelligence.

PHILANTHROPY

We have seen how corporate philanthropy contributed to the success of Ben & Jerry's (pages 79–80) and The Body Shop (pages 83–84), who found that social responsibility could enhance their image—and increase their profits. To maximize the public relations benefits of philanthropy and generate a sense of goodwill among Alpha consumers, businesses should demonstrate a long-term commitment to singular causes that become closely identified with the company; inconsistent philanthropy is likely to have less impact. Of course, if there is a dynamic, high-profile owner (like Anita Roddick of The Body Shop) or chairman (like Ben Cohen of Ben & Jerry's), it may be easier to pursue this strategy than in a company where there are frequent management changes and a myopic focus on the quarterly bottom line.

The selection of philanthropic causes should reflect both the nature of the business and the interests of the Alpha consumer. For example, when The Body Shop supports environmental organizations, it is consistent with the company's eco-aware/natural ingredients/animal rights positioning; when Monsanto touts its work in wildlife preservation, even as it incurs fines from the

Environmental Protection Agency, it merely appears hypocritical. "No one wants to be seen as a socially irresponsible company," says Bob Rosen, a partner in the Washington, D.C., consulting firm Healthy Companies, Inc., so "There's a gap—sometimes a large one—between rhetoric and reality."[12]

In addition to the environment, philanthropic support of education, the arts, AIDS research, and urban renewal programs are likely to generate appreciable goodwill among Alpha consumers. With their respect for knowledge, most of these consumers will respond favorably to educational philanthropy, from Head Start-type programs for children from disadvantaged backgrounds to the endowment of chairs at institutions of higher learning. Support for the arts, from underground film festivals to cultural giants like the New York City Ballet, will appeal to a broad segment of Alpha consumers, whether their interest in the arts is avocational or professional. Their frequent involvement in the arts, entertainment, and visual design fields (all of which have been decimated by AIDS) and their cosmopolitan life-styles have personally exposed many Alpha consumers to the ravages of the disease, so they will appreciate AIDS fund-raising benefits, like "7th On Sale" (in which the Seventh Avenue fashion designers and apparel manufacturers donated merchandise to be sold for the benefit of the New York City AIDS Fund) or "AIDS and Comfort" (in which the Seagram Company and a dozen of San Francisco's top restaurants joined forces to raise money for the local AIDS support agencies). The greatest concentration of Alpha consumers is in major cities, making these people particularly receptive to philanthropy that improves the quality of life in urban America, from isolated contributions like Ben & Jerry's renovation of a New York City subway station to ongoing support of a city's parks.

Philanthropy should be discreet. Businesses should resist the temptation to exploit their charitable contributions. For example, when companies like Philip Morris and Toyota attempt to capitalize on their philanthropy with extensive advertising campaigns extolling their own good deeds, they merely appear self-serving and opportunistic. If your philanthropy is genuine and consistent, Alpha consumers will notice it and appreciate it.

Sponsorships that directly reinforce your business or product are less effective in the eyes of the Alpha consumer than independent no-strings-attached philanthropy. Sponsorships are clearly commercial; when skillfully executed, the perception, at least, of philanthropy is more altruistic. "As soon as you step over the line, you're perceived as a commercial entity," says Peter Meola, vice president and group marketing director of Joseph E. Seagram & Sons, which sponsors a variety of concerts, from the New York Philharmonic to Frank Sinatra.[13] Nevertheless, sponsorships can enhance your brand identity as we saw with Absolut vodka (pages 66–72), Nike (pages 77–78), and Swatch watch (pages 87–88). Other recent examples of innovative corporate sponsorships that complemented their basic business: Perrier "hosted" a series of cabaret performances at the Russian Tea Room in New York (where Perrier is served). Michelob sponsored a concert series at the Ritz in New York featuring many up-and-coming bands, like Jane's Addiction and The Toasters. (Again, Michelob is served at the Ritz.) Barneys New York inaugurated its new store in Tokyo with an art exhibition that included several noted conceptual artists (directly aligning its avante-garde fashions with avante-garde art in the eyes of the consumer). Du Pont and the Intimate Apparel Council sponsored an exhibition and auction of signed works of lingerie-clad models taken by leading fashion photographers (with proceeds from ticket and photography sales going to breast cancer research). Independent consumer research studies that are underwritten by corporations may be another way to reinforce their business in the minds of the trade and the consumer and generate extensive public relations opportunities; the Levi Strauss studies of kids and the Moet & Chandon studies of luxury goods are two excellent examples.

With their strong visual orientation and heightened awareness of semiotics, Alpha consumers are more likely than the mainstream to consciously note products and locales that appear in magazines, movies, and television—with or without accreditation—making product placement an important public relations technique in targeted Alpha marketing. (And even when the product placement is not consciously noted, the subliminal message it delivers can only heighten your brand awareness.) The product placement may appear in editorial, programming, or advertising (for someone else), but it should be a prestigious vehicle that will enhance your brand image. Marketers should be highly selective in their product placement program; indiscriminate placement may actually be counterproductive. For example, a recent episode of ABC's "Roseanne" included a shot of Quaker Oats Squares cereal in Roseanne Barr's kitchen, which might prompt some consumers to associate the product with the down-scale life-style portrayed on the show or with Miss Barr's own considerable girth—in either case, not exactly a purchase incentive for most people. On the other hand, a recent print ad for Judith Leiber handbags featured one of Miss Leiber's products ostensibly photographed on a table at the Le Cirque restaurant in New York (the shot included the bill for the uninitiated); both Judith Leiber and Le Cirque benefited from the mutual association that reinforced their decidedly upscale identities. One of

JUDITH LEIBER PRINT AD
Both Judith Leiber handbags, and Le Cirque benefited from the placement of the restaurant's table-setting (and bill).

the most striking examples of the potential impact of product placement involved a single pair of Bausch and Lomb Wayfarer Ray-Bans sunglasses—the pair that was worn by Tom Cruise in the 1983 film *Risky Business*. The previous year, the company sold about 11,000 pairs of this classic style; after the movie was released, sales increased almost immediately to 4 million pairs, according to Norman Salik, vice president of publicity and promotions.[14]

Although there are various firms and independent contractors specializing in product placement, marketers should consider developing their own product placement program. This will ensure strict product control and minimize costs. (Most product placement brokerage firms charge upwards of $10,000 per placement—and Philip Morris paid $350,000 to have Lark cigarettes featured in the James Bond movie *License To Kill*.[15]) By providing products or locales gratis, it may be possible to gain valuable exposure for your business with a minimal financial investment.

Whatever your public relations strategy, you should have a clear objective in mind and attempt to develop your own criteria for evaluating its efficacy.

CHAPTER 19

___

ADVERTISING

___

As we have noted in our chapters on the Too-Soon-to-Tell case studies (p. 75–85) and Semiotics (p. 113), the decision whether to advertise in a targeted Alpha marketing strategy is difficult to make because the very public nature of advertising can work against the insider's cachet that was characteristic of so many Alpha marketing successes. Among the businesses we analyzed, advertising was the critical success factor in only one: Absolut vodka. In some cases, advertising made a significant contribution to the establishment of a desirable brand identity (e.g., Nike, The Gap, Barneys New York). In others, the advertising had virtually no impact on the Alpha consumer (e.g., Sony, Perrier, Mazda Miata). And in some cases, the absence of advertising only enhanced the product's mystique (e.g., Harley-Davidson, Ben & Jerry's Homemade, The Body Shop). In formulating your advertising strategy, you should address several basic issues.

THE PURCHASE BEHAVIOR OF THE ALPHA CONSUMER

The Alpha consumer regards advertising as a potential source of information—about product attributes, new products, availability, and pricing. If you do not have news or information to convey, the residual benefit of advertising in maintaining top-of-mind awareness may not be worth the investment. Although advertising may trigger memories and associations, it is less likely to stimulate purchase among these very deliberate consumers than among the mainstream, who tend to be less decisive. If an Alpha consumer has tried your product, repurchase will usually be based on product performance, not advertising. For example, all Alpha cola drinkers have tried Coke and Pepsi. Product preference is based on performance, that is, taste; the hundreds of millions of dollars spent on advertising and celebrity endorsements by the two companies involved has little or no impact on Alpha repurchase. If Alpha consumers are already users, stylish advertising that enhances your brand identity may increase their esteem for your business; but if they are not users, advertising alone will not simulate repurchase.

THE NATURE OF YOUR INDUSTRY

In some businesses, such as services that traditionally rely on positive word-of-mouth to build their consumer franchises, advertising may be counterproductive because it suggests to the Alpha consumer that there may be a lack of customer referrals; these businesses range from the medical and legal professions to restaurants and nightclubs. On the other hand, advertising can enhance the credibility of broadly distributed products and services because it suggests that there is sufficient confidence in product quality and sufficient volume to justify an investment in advertising—in other words, quality assurance. These businesses range from automobiles and consumer packaged goods to airlines and banks.

YOUR OBJECTIVES

If you are introducing a new product or service targeted at Alpha consumers, you may want initially to rely on more discreet promotional techniques, such as public relations or direct mail, to reach these opinion leaders and create an insider's cachet for your brand. Once you have developed brand loyalty among Alpha consumers, advertising may help you expand your business among the mainstream. On the other hand, if you are introducing a broadly based product, it may be impossible to build sufficient awareness among the mainstream without advertising.

If you want to establish a "value" positioning or a "green" positioning for your business, the commercial nature of advertising may be counterproductive because Alpha consumers will consider the "hidden" cost hypocritical. (The Alpha consumer knows that she or he is ultimately paying for your advertising.)

If you have news to convey about an existing business—from product improvements to special sales—advertising can be an effective technique. It can also help you reposition your business or update your image, as we saw with The Gap, whose sophisticated "Individuals of Style" print campaign after years of unsophisticated television commercials alerted the Alpha consumer to the company's new merchandising strategy.

Finally, advertising may enhance consumer esteem for your business by demonstrating your sensibility or personality, which contributes to your brand identity, as we saw with the Absolut vodka campaign. According to Bill Hamilton, the creative head of Ogilvy & Mather, "The greatest challenge I face is to make people look forward to ads about a product they really don't care about."[1] In that respect, the Absolut vodka campaign (created by TBWA Advertising) is a remarkable success: even Alpha consumers who are not vodka users "care" about Absolut.

CREATIVE PLATFORM

In developing your creative platform, as with the other elements of your Alpha marketing strategy, it may be instructive to refer to the core values of the Alpha consumer discussed in chapters 1 and 3; if you can strike a responsive chord, you are more likely to attract the attention and interest of this consumer. The following suggestions are some guidelines to follow in creating your advertising strategy, based on Alpha core values.

Information

From the Alpha consumer's perspective, the primary value of advertising is information that will enable him or her to efficiently make a purchase decision; the entertainment that some advertising provides is a minor benefit. Although many Alpha consumers appreciated the inside humor of the celebrated Energizer Bunny advertising campaign from the Eveready Battery Company in 1990, for example, most of them continued to buy Duracell batteries because the Eveready commercials did not provide them with information that would encourage purchase. Alpha consumers were not alone in this respect: Despite a record increase in media spending in 1990 to $28.5 million, Energizer increased its market share only marginally (to 36 percent), whereas Duracell continued to widen its leadership position (to a 44-percent market share.)[2]

The information conveyed in advertising should be consumer benefit-oriented; it should also be meaningful. For example, substantiated product claims are meaningful, but testimonials or self-serving surveys—like the J. D. Power & Associates automobile studies—that invariably provide some type of positive reinforcement, however meritless, for virtually every subscriber, are not. (Even Patricia A. Patano, J. D. Power marketing director, admits that the surveys have become "the claims that ate the industry."[3]) And advertisers should also remember that the Alpha consumer is better informed than the mainstream, making specious advertising claims or inaccuracies extremely risky. For example, when the Chrysler Corporation aired television commercials in 1991 featuring chairman Lee Iacocca extolling the importance of air bags in cars, savvy Alpha consumers who had read the business press or Mr. Iacocca's best-selling autobiography published in 1984 (not to mention the Doonesbury political cartoon created by Gary Trudeau) were not impressed, because they knew that Mr. Iacocca had publicly opposed air bags for years. Similarly, literate Alpha consumers were bemused when a 1990 television commercial for Calvin Klein's Obsession fragrance, a product with a highly sexual positioning, featured an ironic quote from the Jake Barnes character in Hemingway's *The Sun Also Rises*—ironic because Jake Barnes was impotent.

Cosmopolitanism

The cosmopolitan characteristic of Alpha consumers enables them to relate to various sensibilities. Advertising with a distinct point of view is more likely to appeal to them than a generalized approach. For example, if the advertising includes images of product users, the depiction of a narrow, but realistic, customer franchise is likely to be more effective than a generic life-style campaign designed to appeal to everyone. Similarly, music that makes a statement, whether it is country, opera, Kurt Weill, or reggae, is preferable to the generic pop music favored by most advertisers. The Alpha consumer's individual preferences are incidental; he or she will respect your conviction.

Communication

The goal of advertising should be the clear communication of product benefits to the consumer; it should not be designed to entertain or win creative awards. Advertising is a sales technique, not an art form. In a 1991 interview, David Ogilvy, the founder of Ogilvy and Mather, said, "I want to sell products, but advertising people today, they want to win awards. They use advertising to promote themselves, so they can get better jobs and higher salaries. It's a scandal."[4] Dan Wieden, president of the Weiden & Kennedy advertising agency, which has received many industry awards for its unorthodox campaigns for Nike, explains why his agency refuses to join the American Association of Advertising Agencies, the industry's primary trade organization: "I don't belong to the 4 As and I have no intention to. I don't mean this as arrogant, but I really don't care what the industry thinks of us. That's the wrong drummer to be marching to." Mr. Wieden adds that some of his agency's "best work has never been applauded by the industry and some of our worst work has. We're trying to make ourselves valid to our clients."[5] The recent closing of the award-winning boutique agency Buckley/DeCerchio/Cavalier, considered one of Madison Avenue's hot creative shops, provides further confirmation that awards do not sell products. Former creative director Tom DeCerchio admits "the things you win awards with ... don't make any money."[6]

Moreover, Edward de Bono, an authority on creative and conceptual thinking cautions that "Advertisers should be communicators, not creators. . . . Creative people rarely make good communicators. . . . The reason is that their 'logical in hindsight' may be highly individual."[7] Today, truly creative people tend to gravitate to the fields of design, entertainment, and the arts where they have greater freedom to pursue their individual visions. And those who do become involved in advertising often leave the industry in frustration. The defection from Madison Avenue to Hollywood is particularly striking, from Adrian Lyne, who abandoned commercials to direct feature films, like *Fatal Attraction* and *9-1/2 Weeks*, to Mr. DeCerchio, who is abandoning copywriting for screenwriting.

Every advertiser must determine what message it wants to communicate to consumers and carefully evaluate proposed creative platforms within that context. The automotive industry, for example, spends $6 billion a year on advertising in the United States. Unfortunately, in most cases, the communication of product benefits is unclear, seriously undermining the investment in advertising. If one examines the copy platforms of some current automobile campaigns, it is hardly surprising that new car sales are declining:

- I love what you do for me (Toyota)
- Built for the human race (Nissan)
- It just feels right (Mazda)
- The heartbeat of America (Chevrolet)

If you can provide consumers with no more compelling reason to purchase your car than telling them that it is "for humans" or "made in America" (when most people associate inferior quality with American-made cars), you should probably not waste your money on advertising. A recently published study by Fred Mannering and Clifford Winston involving nearly 500 households and their vehicle purchases over several decades confirms that Americans are now more loyal to Japanese brands than to American ones.[8] Of course, copy is only one aspect of communication; audio and visual semiotics in advertising are equally important. In targeting Alpha consumers, particular attention should be paid to subtle nuances. For example, props and locations can provide key visual cues to your identity. When the model in an Estée Lauder cosmetics ad holds a bottle of Evian water or the model in a Paramount Hotel ad is reading Jack Kerouac, it sends a distinct message to Alpha consumers and contributes to an insider's cachet. Similarly, a Liz Claiborne hosiery ad featuring a model photographed in front of the Empire Diner in New York or a Katherine Hamnett ad featuring a man and a woman in what is clearly a public restroom demonstrates a hip sensibility that the Alpha consumer can relate to.

Originality

In theory, original advertising that positions the product in a unique and unforgettable way that will establish a distinctive brand identity in the minds of consumers should be the goal. In reality, the challenge of creating original advertising in an industry where genuine innovation can become a cliché overnight may not be possible without forfeiting your purpose, that is, selling the product. In general, consistency is more important than originality in advertising. It may be more effective to update your current campaign than introduce a new one. Despite literally hundreds of imitators, two highly original print campaigns—the "Absolut _____" campaign for Absolut vodka (introduced in 1980) and the "Perception/Reality" campaign for *Rolling Stone* magazine (introduced in 1986)—have remained fresh and distinctive by consistently updating their basic creative platforms. The value of consistency in advertising was revealed in a recent study conducted by Video Storyboard Tests, Inc., which tracks advertising popularity among consumers: Among the top 10 print campaigns for 1990, most are at least 3 years old and several (including Absolut vodka) have been running for a decade. "Consistency and continuity—that's the secret for magazines if you want to be visible," says Dick Costello, president of Absolut's agency, TBWA.[9]

In pursuit of originality, advertisers are often "inspired" by creative developments in other fields, such as movies or fashion design. They should proceed with caution, however, because the objectives and sensibility may be entirely different. For example, in the November 1986 issue of *The Face*, the hip British magazine, a fashion editorial featured a virtual chorus line of eccentric-looking people parading through various urban settings wearing the clothes of Jean Paul Gaultier. Gaultier is an avant-garde designer and *The Face* is an avant-garde publication, so

this approach worked. However, when Reebok International slav-
ishly copied this editorial two years later in its short-lived
"U.B.U." advertising campaign, created by Chiat/Day/Mojo in
New York, it was an inappropriate approach for marketing athletic shoes, and the campaign—and the agency—were quickly
changed.

Involvement

Like most other consumers today, Alphas selectively pay attention to advertising. "People are bombarded with ads, and they
have developed significant, sophisticated methods of selecting
which ads to watch," says Alex Biel, a psychologist and former
head of the Ogilvy Center for Research and Development, an
advertising institute that recently closed. "Otherwise, we'd all be
in rubber rooms."[10] However, if you can successfully attract the
attention of the analytical Alpha consumer, he or she is more
likely than his or her mainstream counterpart to become involved
in your advertising. Campaigns that constitute a series or vari-
ations on a theme may actually prompt Alphas to watch for your
latest ad. In addition to Absolut vodka and *Rolling Stone* magazine, this approach has been successfully employed by American
Express ("Cardmember since _____"), Parliament Lights
cigarettes ("The perfect recess"), and Jim Beam Kentucky
Straight Bourbon Whiskey ("You always come back to the
basics"), among others. Similarly, advertising campaigns featuring wordplay (e.g., NYNEX "If it's out there . . ."), uniden-
tified spokespersons (e.g., Blackglama mink "What becomes a
legend most"), or people likely to be recognized by the Alpha
consumer but not the general public (e.g., The Gap "Individuals
of Style") can encourage involvement, not unlike solving a puzzle.

Identity

Advertising identity should be based on an understanding of who
you are, not necessarily who you would like to be. You should
recognize that you cannot be all things to all people; an indistinct
identity designed to appeal to everyone is unlikely to appeal to
anyone. You may have to risk alienating some consumers to max-

imize your appeal to your target customer. Ed McCabe, Madison Avenue's prodigal son, says, "If you don't shake some people up negatively, you're not getting anybody positively."[11] The "United Colors of Benetton" campaign, for example, which has consistently featured provocative images of everything from interracial couples to condoms has created a distinctive visual language that appeals to some while incensing others.

If your company markets various products or services under different brand names, you will have to decide whether you want to emphasize your corporate identity or your brand identity. In general, if you are marketing related products or services, it may be most efficient to develop equity in your corporate identity. In the athletic shoe category, for example, Nike has always emphasized its corporate identity; consequently most of the Nike advertising has a "halo" effect on the company's other products. Converse, on the other hand, has marketed its brands separately, substantially diluting the equity in the Converse name. (Nike's share of the $5.5-billion athletic shoe market has increased to 24 percent, and the Converse share has declined to 2 percent.[12]) On the other hand, if you are marketing unrelated products or niche brands within the same category, it may be more effective to emphasize the brand identity; this approach has been successfully employed by companies as diverse as Procter & Gamble and Estée Lauder.

Coop or omnibus advertising featuring multiple advertisers is risky. It seldom enhances your brand identity—and frequently dilutes it. You must never allow someone else to control your image; if omnibus advertising is required in your industry, make certain that you are involved in its creation.

In determining your identity, or positioning, several issues should be addressed:

• Advertising is most effective when your identity is self-defined; that is, when you do not include extraneous references, whether it is a celebrity spokesperson or a competitive product. You then "own" your positioning; you appear to be above the competitive fray; and you provide consumers with a unique reason to buy your product.

• Comparative advertising is dangerous because it places you in a defensive posture. "It's risky and has a tendency to flop," says Tedd Sann, the BBDO vice chairman who has been involved in the creation of some of the Pepsi comparative advertising.[13] Comparative advertising is only valid when you can provide a positive reason to choose your product—not a negative reason not to purchase your competitor's product. In general, comparative advertising based on factual product features, whether it involves mileage-per-gallon, ingredients, or price, is more effective in influencing Alpha purchase behavior than subjective criteria, like "independent" consumer taste tests. And if you plan to pursue a comparative advertising strategy, make certain that your comparison is a factor in Alpha purchase motivation; if your argument is irrelevant, your advertising may actually stimulate purchase of your competitor's product, which you have so generously featured in your ad.

• If a spokesperson is going to represent your identity to consumers, the spokesperson should be appropriate, exclusive, accessible, and long term. Product creators or designers, like Paloma Picasso, or historically documented product users, like the American Express cardmembers, are the most appropriate. Possible or potential product users, like the people who appear in The Gap "Individuals of Style" campaign, are somewhat less appropriate. And egotistical corporate managers, like Victor Kiam for Remington, or celebrities who are patently nonusers, like vegetarian actress Cybill Shepherd for the Beef Industry Council, are not only inappropriate, they seriously damage your credibility.

• Spokespersons should be exclusive; celebrities with multiproduct endorsements, from Lauren Bacall to Joe Montana, suggest a lack of commitment to your business and tend to confuse consumers. *Question*: What do the following people have in common—Steve Guttenberg, Paula Abdul, Arsenio Hall, Joe Montana, Billy Crystal, Vanilla Ice, Demi Moore, Bruce Willis, Fred Savage, Leslie Nielsen, Mike Tyson, Don Johnson, Madonna, Kirk Cameron, Ray Charles, Michael Jordan, MC Hammer, Michael J. Fox, New Kids On The Block, and the two Mr. Jacksons, Michael and Bo? (Do you know? Do you care?) *Answer*: They are among the celebrities who have appeared in Coke and/or Pepsi commercials in recent years. Now, if you can just correctly match each celebrity with the cola brand(s) he or she

endorsed ... Dave Vadhera, editor of Video Storyboard Tests'
newsletter *Commercial Break* confirmed that recall studies in-
dicated that there was total confusion among consumers.[14] *The
bottom line*: In the past 10 years, neither company has been able
to significantly change its market share—Coca-Cola still has
about a 41 percent share of the $44-billion soft drink market;
Pepsi-Cola still has about a 30 percent share.[15] Jay Coleman,
president of the entertainment marketing firm Rockbill adds
"Getting a [commercial] virgin is very important to an advertiser
... The first-time commercial affiliation has built-in publicity
and awareness."[16]

• Spokespersons should be long term. Businesses should
consider following the lead of companies like Nike and Cosmair
who sign up-and-coming athletes and actresses to long-term con-
tracts and let the product make them celebrities whose identification with the product is complete in the minds of consumers.
When Nike signed Michael Jordan in 1985 (for Air Jordans) and
Cosmair signed Isabella Rossellini in 1982 (for Lancôme), each
was a promising, but unproven, property; their subsequent
professional success has produced a highly synergistic benefit for
the companies they represent. As *Adweek* critic Barbara Lippert
points out, "The Lancôme campaign featuring Isabella Rossellini
conveys a sense of a real person who grows in her own life while
keeping her long-standing relationship with one company."[17]

Finally, we should note some fundamental caveats regarding
spokespersons. First, there is an inherent conflict in the minds
of Alpha consumers regarding paid endorsements and the integrity of the spokesperson. As Jon Pareles, pop music critic for
the *New York Times*, explains, "Everyone is diminished by endorsements. Look at David Bowie: After he endorsed Pepsi, he
never did anything good again. It's the reason Bette Midler
sued. ... Once you see a 'For Sale' sign, you can't take it back."
(Mr. Pareles is a purist; he even objects to voice-overs: "When
I hear Phoebe Snow doing voice-overs, *I* know it's her, and it
makes me sad.") Moreover, a fundamental shift in social values
has further weakened the credibility of celebrity spokespersons.
Novelist and critic Jon Katz explains: "In the eighties, when
money was all over, celebrity didn't seem as grotesque as it does
now. [Today] it just seems tasteless and inappropriate." In their

insatiable quest for new celebrities, the media—and advertisers—also have considerably lowered their standards. (Even Donna Rice, whose only claim to fame was her sexual relationship with Gary Hart, had an endorsement.) Mr. Katz adds, "Celebrity became cheap. It's been devalued. It doesn't count to be a celebrity anymore."[18]

Second, the potential danger always exists that the spokesperson will become a source of embarrassment due to the vagaries of fortune or the increasing media scrutiny of anyone in the public eye. "You can't fool anybody anymore," says public relations veteran Lee Solters. "You'll be found out."[19]

Third, media coverage of actual users always carries more credibility than an endorsement featured in advertising. For example, when avant-garde theatrical director Peter Sellars wore a white Gap dress shirt in the company's "Individuals of Style" campaign in 1989, the ad attracted the attention of certain Alpha consumers—and may even have stimulated purchase; after all, there was no reason to believe that Mr. Sellars would not wear the shirt. However, Mr. Sellar's confession in a subsequent printed interview that he wears Brooks Brothers shirts made a much greater impact on Alpha consumers than his paid Gap endorsement ("When I wear those kinds of shirts, I wear Brooks Brothers. They're cut really big, which is great. And I hate shopping, so I don't spend any time doing it ever. So this is great, because you know that you can get a shirt in 25 seconds and not really think about it very much.")[20]

Last, the next time that someone proposes the use of a spokesperson, try to analyze her or his motivation. More often than not, it reflects personal aspirations rather than a sound marketing rationale. (Whenever a celebrity is involved, it is amazing how many people—from both the client and agency camps—find that they absolutely must be present at the shoot.)

Consider a few final thoughts regarding your identity or positioning:

• Aspirational advertising is the wrong psychological tactic to take when targeting Alpha consumers; if you have to claim cachet, you clearly do not have it. Some of the most flagrant examples include companies that attempt to achieve cachet by association with status symbols. When Lincoln Continental

("What a luxury car should be") aligns itself with Fabergé ("What an egg should be") or Sevres ("What a jug should be"), it is wildly inappropriate. (It is also ill-conceived: To evoke fragile, antique porcelain when attempting to sell a new car is ludicrous, even for the most aspirational consumer.)

• Humorous advertising is risky unless something is inherently funny about your product, such as an entertainment property. Although humorous advertising is frequently memorable, it seldom stimulates purchase; for most consumers, there is nothing particularly funny about spending their money regardless of the purchase. Many Alpha consumers found "Lying Joe," the Isuzu salesman, amusing, but hardly persuasive; despite heavy media investment (in 1990, Isuzu spent $636 per car on media while Honda spent just $270), Isuzu sales continued to decline, and the campaign—and the agency—were replaced in 1991.[21]

• Advertising that parodies other advertising demonstrates a bankruptcy of creativity and a self-indulgence unlikely to appeal to Alpha consumers (who are not as fascinated with advertising as Madison Avenue would like to believe). As *Advertising Age* critic Bob Garfield points out, "Self-consciousness is a poor substitute for substance. If you have nothing important to say and no fetching way to say it, better hire a blimp with Your Logo Here."[22]

Self-Sufficiency

To satisfy the Alpha consumer's sense of self-sufficiency, advertising should provide enough information to enable her or him to make a purchase decision or, at least, to seek additional information. Devices that provide additional information, such as the inclusion of a toll-free information number in the advertising, may enable you to capitalize on interest generated by your advertising. In 1989, for example, *The New Yorker* reported that the inclusion of toll-free numbers generated some 25,000 inquiries to 100 of its advertisers.[23]

Media Planning

The strong print orientation among Alpha consumers should inform the media plan of any targeted advertising campaign.

These consumers read a variety of publications and frequently tear out ads for future investigation or purchase.

With a few notable exceptions, such as CBS's "Sixty Minutes," most Alpha consumers do not watch sufficient network television to justify an investment in network time. While acknowledging her print bias, most Alphas would agree with *Vanity Fair* editor Tina Brown when she described the TV networks as "square, cowardly, bland, repetitive, and deeply unsatisfying."[24] If Alphas watch television, it is generally cable or PBS.

Radio may be cost-effective if you have "news" about existing businesses that have already achieved a high level of awareness; the news may be anything from sales to up-coming concerts. Due to its single dimension, radio is a less successful medium for building brand awareness or creating a distinctive brand identity. As with their television viewing, Alphas favor specialized radio programming, such as college, urban black, classical, or all-news formats.

Outdoor advertising is paradoxical. Alphas consider billboards a blight on the landscape, but they like the renegade appeal of illegally placed posters, which are frequently associated with rock concerts and the underground.

In planning your Alpha media strategy, keep in mind that these influential consumers represent no more than 5 percent of the total population; consequently, your media selection should be guided by editorial quality, not demographics.

CHAPTER 20

PROMOTION

The decisive purchase behavior of Alpha consumers makes them less responsive than the mainstream to promotion. This is supported by research studies, which indicate that educated consumers who want a lot of product information before they buy tend not to react quickly to promotions.[1] With the notable exception of sampling or trial (which frequently results in purchase when the product or service offers a distinctive competitive advantage), most promotional marketing, at best, represents "added value" or "entertainment" in the eyes of the Alpha consumer, but it is seldom sufficient incentive to stimulate purchase. Many promotional techniques may actually diminish consumer esteem for your business.

In the case studies we explored, promotion was never a critical success factor. Indeed, the absence of overt promotion, such as discounting and premiums, contributed to the success of many businesses, from Absolut vodka to Chanel. Although Alpha consumers appreciated the entertainment provided by imaginative promotions, like Ben & Jerry's Cowmobile and MTV's John Cougar Mellencamp "Paint the Mother Pink" contest, they felt betrayed when Izod Lacoste appeared in discount stores and Perrier coupons materialized in Sunday newspaper inserts.

PROMOTIONAL PLANNING

In planning a promotional strategy, marketers should address several basic issues.
* Promotion diminishes the perceived value of your business

and contributes to a commodity mentality that discourages brand loyalty. Michael Smith, assistant professor of marketing at Temple University's School of Business and Management, succinctly describes promotion as "an excuse to buy your product, not a reason."[2] Joe Plummer, an executive vice president at the D'Arcy Masius Benton & Bowles advertising agency, adds, "Marketers have brought this on themselves with their heavy use of promotions. Without some real product improvements, it's going to be difficult to win that loyalty back."[3]

• Price promotion jeopardizes your brand image. James Lattin, associate professor of marketing and management science at the Stanford University Graduate School of Business explains, "Through advertising, you try to convince people to value your product enough to want to pay for it. With price promotions, you teach them to buy it for less. There's a sense that these promotions undermine the investment that companies make in their brand names."[4]

• Promotion is not a sustainable competitive advantage when everyone does it. Moreover, it creates future consumer expectations that damage the entire industry. From rebates in the automobile industry to frequent-flyer programs in the airline business to premiums in the upscale fragrance market, we have seen how institutionalized promotion can diminish profitability for everyone involved.

With increasingly short product life cycles, marketers should focus on the bottom line, not volume; it is better to sacrifice the short-term increase in volume generated by expensive promotional techniques to protect the bottom line.

The most effective promotions are proprietary, integrated, and multilayered. They stimulate purchase while effectively reinforcing the brand's long-term marketing objectives, including its positioning, distribution, and advertising strategies.

Following are some promotional techniques and their impact on Alpha consumer behavior.

SAMPLING AND TRIAL

Sampling or trial is the most persuasive type of promotion if you can demonstrate superior product performance or a distinct differential advantage. Alpha consumers love to try new products, and they respect businesses with sufficient confidence in the quality of their product or service to encourage sampling or trial. However, if your product represents parity, or inferior, quality, sampling may be counterproductive because you will sacrifice even that trial purchase.

Sampling is generally most productive when you are introducing a new product, whether you are targeting professional Alphas (Fuji film made significant inroads into the influential professional photographers market, long dominated by Kodak, when it gave free film to photographers shooting the Olympic Games in 1984, of which it was a sponsor)[5] or a broader consumer base (in 1991 television commercials featuring a toll-free 800 number, Johnson & Johnson offered a free pair of its new disposable contact lenses available through optometrists). The opportunity to sample new products that are not yet available for purchase, or are available in very limited distribution channels, can also create a sense of consumer demand that will generate important word-of-mouth and build brand awareness; this strategy has been successfully employed by fragrance companies, like Calvin Klein Cosmetics, who "preview" new products via scented inserts in image-building magazines prior to retail introduction. (When the company introduced the Escape fragrance for women in 1991, for example, 40 million scent strips were inserted in magazines one month before the product was available in stores.)

Sampling should be tightly controlled; random sampling diminishes the consumer's perception of product value and exclusivity. It may be better to give the consumer an "invitation" to be redeemed for a "complimentary gift" than to arbitrarily distribute a free sample. We have seen how the indiscriminate distribution of free copies of *Spy* magazine in Manhattan apartment building lobbies contributed to its downfall. Whether sampling takes place in retail stores, amenity programs, or special events, the environment should enhance your image. For example, Absolut vodka reinforces its upscale identity with sampling at glamorous charity benefits.

FREQUENCY PROGRAMS

Frequency programs alone will not motivate the Alpha consumer to patronize your business if your product or service performance is unsatisfactory. However, when product performance is acceptable, frequency programs can contribute to brand loyalty. Airline frequent-flyer and compact disk and book clubs are good examples of frequency programs that represent added-value in the minds of Alpha consumers. Nonprice awards, such as Visa programs, which contribute one free mile of airline travel for every dollar charged on the consumer's Visa credit card, are better than cash rebates for several reasons: You are less likely to diminish the perceived value of your basic product or service; you can offer the consumer better value for the promotion dollar; and nonprice awards have greater remembrance value, unlike money, which is quickly spent and forgotten.

SPECIAL OFFERS

When properly presented, special offers enable you to assume a promotional posture without compromising the integrity of your basic business; special offers permit you to enhance the perceived value of your product on a limited basis without resorting to destructive devices, like discounting and premiums. The special offer may involve an ancillary product or service that complements yours; for example, for a Valentine's Day promotion in 1991, Steuben offered beautiful floral arrangements delivered in one of its distinctive crystal vases. The offer may represent a special size that will encourage trial purchase or novelty packaging that will maximize sales among your existing customer franchise; this approach has been successfully employed by Pepsi Cola with its promotional cans. If you are in a service industry, offer a variation of your basic product; for example, in the summer of 1989, restauranteur Pino Luongo imported a half dozen

LE MADRI RESTAURANT IN NEW YORK
Owner Pino Luongo, with his Italian "mammas" in 1989. The successful
promotion generated considerable interest among consumer and the
media.

Italian "mammas" with no professional restaurant experience to
work in the kitchen of Le Madri, his trendy Italian restaurant
in New York, and showcase regional specialties passed down
through generations from mother to daughter. ("No matter that
two of the women were neither married nor mothers and that
one lived in Brooklyn, where she ran a catering business," noted
Bryan Miller in the *New York Times*. "It made for a public
relations bonanza."[6]) As with other types of promotion, special
offers are only effective when they are, indeed, special, so businesses should utilize them sparingly.

SPECIAL EVENTS

Like advertising, special events have reached a saturation point, substantially reducing their marketing efficacy. According to the International Events Group, American marketers spend more than $2 billion a year on special events, making it increasingly difficult to break through the clutter.[7] A successful special event is memorable, if not always unique, and reinforces the brand positioning. In Alpha target marketing, special events may enhance your brand image and create awareness, but they seldom generate immediate purchase.

Their inability to advertise on television appears to have stimulated many liquor companies to develop innovative special events (which often succeed in generating television media coverage that proves more valuable than commercials). Heublein, for example, sponsors the Cuervo Gold Crown, three professional volleyball tournaments that closely align the tequila brand with the hip beach life-style in the minds of consumers and generate tremendous media coverage at the same time. In promoting Breezers, its new line of "spirits-based coolers," Bacardi Imports has sponsored "tastings" in summer resort areas up and down the East and West Coast and in liquor stores throughout the country. When Breezers were introduced in 10 markets in 1989, the product was the 52nd-largest selling liquor brand in the country by total case sales; in 1990, the company sold more than 4 million cases of Breezers, making it the 3rd-largest selling liquor brand.[8]

CROSS-PROMOTIONS AND TIE-INS

Cross-promotions and tie-ins should be logical, mutually beneficial, and offer the consumer added value; ill-conceived cross-promotions should be avoided because they jeopardize your brand identity. For example, cross-promotions between airlines, hotels, and car rental companies are logical, mutually beneficial, and offer the consumer added value; but when Continental Airlines offers a "complimentary" $25 gift certificate at Lord & Taylor as a purchase incentive for airline tickets, it makes little sense because travel and retailing are unrelated industries.

Cross-promotions can be particularly beneficial for small businesses, which lack the awareness and financial resources to justify their own promotions. When Uncle Dave's Kitchen, a small gourmet food company in Vermont, wanted to promote its Bloody Mary mix, it went to the importers of Absolut Vodka with a cross-promotion concept: mixing the world's biggest Bloody Mary. In return for the idea, Uncle Dave's Bloody Mary Fixin's was named cosponsor of the event, although Absolut paid most of the promotional costs. J. B. Lyon, president of Uncle Dave's Kitchen, gratefully acknowledged, "Working with a multi-million-dollar company, they understood our position."[9] During the run of *Henry IV, Parts 1 and 2* at the Public Theater in New York in 1991, eight relatively small restaurants in the neighborhood, including the ultrahip Indochine and Flamingo East, gave customers a 10-percent discount when they presented their theater ticket stub. Most consumers combine dinner and evening entertainment, making restaurants and theaters complementary businesses, so this approach worked.

Unless you are marketing an entertainment property with a very short product life cycle, you should not license your brand name for cross-promotional products; the damage to your brand image is not worth the additional exposure or incremental royalties it might generate. When the Walt Disney Company signed 30 licensees to support the release of *The Rocketeer* in 1991, it was a valid promotional technique because most films have short product life cycles; when the Pepsi-Cola Company licensed the Diet Pepsi advertising imagery and copy platform ("You've got the right one baby, uh-huh") to United Brands International in 1991 for a line of budget-priced apparel to be sold in stores like J. C. Penney, it was a short-sighted dilution of their brand equity. (Had the company already forgotten the Pepsi apparel fiasco of the 1980s?)

PRICE PROMOTION

Seasonal price promotions or sales are appropriate for seasonal merchandise, from apparel to sports equipment, or for discontinued items; consumers can understand the rationale. However, frequent discounting of regular products or services only diminishes the consumer's perception of value and creates future price expectations that cannot be sustained without undermining profitability. William Whyte, an analyst with Stephens Inc. explains, "If a retailer has an item at 40 percent off this week, the customer thinks 'Why wasn't it 40 percent off last week?' Are they raping, robbing and pillaging all year?"[10] Businesses must be willing to sacrifice the short-term increase in volume that discounting may generate to protect their image—and safeguard long-term profitability. Brooks Brothers, for example, the nation's oldest clothing store, deviated from its traditional seasonal sales strategy once in 1990 with spectacular results: Charge card customers were offered a 25-percent discount on any item in the store—and the company experienced one of the biggest monthly sales increases in its history. However, management recognized the danger of discounting; they did not repeat the promotion. "We still needed the business, but we decided that we did not want to be a promotional store," said William V. Roberti, the company's president and chief executive.[11] This approach should enable Brooks Brothers to remain above the competitive fray. (In 1990, more than 65 percent of all men's dress shirts were sold at discount according to the Market Research Corporation. "That's not what we spent over 100 years building a brand for," lamented Lawrence S. Phillips, chairman and chief executive of the Phillips-Van Heusen Corporation and great grandson of the company's founder.)[12]

If businesses want to stimulate sales during a certain period of time, instead of discounting, they should donate a specified amount of sales to charity. The impact on the bottom line will be the same as discounting, but the perception among consumers will be quite different. Price discounting destroys your image; charitable donations enhance it. Your charitable contribution policy should be explicit, whether it involves a specified percentage of sales or profits, or a fixed donation for each transaction; for example, in March 1991, Cartier donated 10 percent of retail sales in all of its 130 boutiques to the Red Cross.[13] Indefinite contribution policies cause consumers to question your commitment, and they are unlikely to respond; for example, Bloomingdale's promise in 1991 to donate "the greater portion of profits" from its "Red Hot and Blue" shop to AIDS research was simply too vague to motivate purchase.[14]

COUPONS

Alpha consumers rarely respond to coupons; the value they represent is not worth the inconvenience. Moreover, if you want to create a quality image for your brand, you should not run coupon promotions. With an average 3-percent redemption rate today,[15] the incremental sales increases a coupon might generate are not worth the damage to your image. (Between 1980 and 1986, coupon distribution increased by more than 124 percent, substantially reducing their efficacy; A. C. Nielsen reports that more than 200 billion coupons are now distributed each year.)[16] We saw how coupons in Sunday newspaper supplements adversely affected the upscale identity that Perrier had so carefully cultivated. However, if coupons are a standard practice in your category, there are ways to mitigate their negative impact on your brand image. First, devote the same kind of creative attention to coupons that product design and advertising receive; after all, a coupon is essentially an advertisement for your product. Second, do not insult the consumer with a redemption value under one dollar regardless of your price-point; anything less is contemptuous of the consumer's time. Finally, clearly differentiate your coupon with a freestanding insert or an independent direct mail offer; for example, in Sunday newspapers, Procter & Gamble recently ran a freestanding, two-sided insert printed on glossy, high-quality paper that was basically an 8-1/2″ × 11″ replica of the distinctive Tide detergent box. And General Mills mailed an attractive 5″ × 9″ postcard featuring Oatmeal Crisp/Oatmeal Raisin Crisp cereals that similarly reinforced the package design.

PREMIUMS

Premiums seldom influence Alpha consumers. When investing, they want the highest rate of return, not a "free" TV set; when purchasing fragrance, they want cologne, not a "free" set of wine glasses. However, if premiums are part of your marketing strategy, they should in some way enhance either your brand image or the use of your product. For example, when Clinique features a "bonus" containing a selection of travel-sized Clinique products, they offer the consumer a unique premium with perceived value while encouraging sampling at the same time. On the other hand, when Chemical Bank in New York offers consumers who deposit $5000 in a "Select Banking" account such decidedly unselect "gifts" as a free hot-dog at Nathan's Famous, they seriously undermine their credibility.

In general, the most appealing premiums are either unique items that the consumer cannot obtain elsewhere (like the Clinique product gifts) or utilitarian items that nearly everyone can use (like umbrellas). Premiums that are essentially public relations gifts or teasers—in other words, premiums that are not contingent upon purchase—are more effective than gift-with-purchase and purchase-with-purchase promotions because they generate goodwill without devaluing your product.

CONTESTS AND SWEEPSTAKES

Alpha consumers do not enter contests or sweepstakes; they are too realistic about the opportunities to win to waste their time. Consequently, an innovative contest theme or a unique grand prize that will reflect your taste and enhance your brand identity is more important than investing millions of dollars in multiple prizes. During the summer of 1991, both Coca-Cola and Sperry Top-Sider ran promotions featuring convertibles. Coca-Cola awarded $74 million in prizes, including 130 new convertibles;[17] Sperry Top-Sider awarded a single 1953 Corvette. Needless to say, Alpha consumers were more impressed by the Corvette. As with special events, imaginative contests can also provide entertainment value, even if they do not elicit participation or stimulate purchase. The MTV network's Nickelodeon/Nick at Nite cable channel, for example, ran a Halloween promotion in 1990 that included a marathon broadcast of 140 episodes of "Alfred Hitchcock Presents," a "Dead Giveaway" contest with a toll-free number to predict the number of screen fatalities viewers would see, and Mr. Hitchcock's profile, 300 feet high, looming over New York and Los Angeles.[18]

CHAPTER 21

GREEN MARKETING

With the accelerated rate of change in the 20th century, broad sociological trends are increasingly defined in terms of decades, rather than centuries. The 1960s were Radical Chic; the 1970s were the Me Decade; the 1980s were Greed; and we will call the 1990s the Green Decade (until Tom Wolfe gets around to officially naming it). Our definition of the Green sensibility is quite broad: Anything involving body, mind, and spirit that improves the quality of life for the individual or for the planet. Today, nearly all Americans do something that may be included in the green canon, creating many new opportunities for a green marketing approach.

Alpha consumers have characteristically been at the forefront of the green movement, which went through a somewhat esoteric and spiritual stage in the 1980s involving channeling, crystals, Reiki, and other phenomena unlikely to gain mainstream consumer acceptance; in the pragmatic 1990s, the movement has quite literally come down to earth with a focus on the environment and holistic health. More and more people are recognizing the impact of their emotional and mental state on their physical health, and they are taking steps to prevent illness, foster wellness, and promote longevity. Much of this holistic health approach is based on ancient Eastern principles of self-awareness that treat the mind and body as one; with the establishment of psychoneuroimmunology, modern medicine is beginning to move in this direction. Many of the people who are assuming self-responsibility for their health and well-being have a heightened sense of social responsibility that is also peculiarly oriental in its acknowledgment of the fundamental connection between the individual, society, and the environment. These consumers are increasingly voting with their pocketbooks by patronizing businesses that correspond to their values (and effectively boycotting those businesses that do not).

Green marketing will become a consumer hot button of the 1990s. Already embraced by the most influential consumers—Alphas, the affluent, the young—it is only a matter of time before it reaches the mainstream. (McDonald's introduction of "healthy" cuisine—like green salads, the McLean Burger, and potatoes fried in vegetable oil—and its elimination of polystyrene containers in response to shifting consumer demands suggests that it already has.) We have seen how Ben and Jerry's Homemade Inc. (p. 79-80) and The Body Shop (p. 83-84) successfully executed green marketing strategies with an emphasis on natural ingredients, environmental responsibility, corporate philanthropy—and an absence of advertising, which is inherently ungreen in its commercialism; this approach fostered an emotional bond with the consumer and contributed to the brands' insider cachet. Large companies that traditionally rely on expensive advertising and promotion techniques may have difficulty adjusting to the concept of green marketing. John Scott, executive vice president/executive creative director at J. Walter Thompson in Detroit, who handled the account for Kellogg's Mueslix, a breakfast cereal with a natural positioning, discovered, "When you try old-fashioned hard-sell methods to sell these products, you don't get anywhere."[1] And Mark Egide, general manager of Carmex Inc., which purchased Mill Creek Natural Products from Procter & Gamble's Richardson-Vicks division in 1987, asserts that the packaged goods giant "lost a ton of money because they spent so much on marketing" including a multimillion dollar print advertising campaign.[2] But even companies that have difficulty adjusting to the low-key approach should have little difficulty with the relatively low cost of green marketing.

STRATEGIC PLANNING

In formulating a green marketing strategy, businesses should begin by promoting whatever they presently do that conforms to the green sensibility, whether it involves product, packaging, operations, or philanthropy; this will help them deflect the appearance of green marketing opportunism. In marketing its o.b. tampon, for example, the Personal Products Corporation, a division of Johnson & Johnson, is capitalizing on the product's lack of a plastic applicator, converting a potential disadvantage into an environmental asset. Businesses must then correct or improve practices that are inconsistent with green marketing. When Playtex Family Products Corporation, for example, repackaged its Jhirmack line of haircare products in 1991, they eliminated the outer packaging, saving 800 tons of paperboard annually and substantially reducing their manufacturing costs while demonstrating their eco-awareness. Finally, businesses should demonstrate a sustained commitment to green marketing with sponsorship of environmental, educational, and philanthropic programs. Patagonia, Inc., for example, an outdoor clothing manufacturer, contributes 10 percent of its before-tax profits to environmental groups.[3]

In identifying green marketing opportunities, businesses should anticipate developments among consumers, competitors, and regulatory commissions; green marketing is more effective when it appears to be progressive rather than defensive. Following are a few examples of developments among consumers that are creating green marketing opportunities (and potential problems for businesses that fail to respond):

• The back-to-nature movement is sparking a renewed interest in gardening and outdoor activities, like fishing, hiking, and camping (which has shown a steady increase over the past four years according to the U.S. Travel Data Center).[4]

• The rising birth rate is creating demand for diaper services, which have grown 250 percent in recent years, as consumers increasingly reject disposable diapers.

• The growing resistance to automobile traffic and air pollution is leading many consumers to bicycles, mass transit, and carpooling.

• The appeal of natural products that are free of chemicals is causing some consumers to return to simple household cleaning products, like vinegar and baking soda. (Sales increases of Heinz white vinegar in gallon sizes and Arm & Hammer baking soda have doubled in recent years.)[5]

• The desire for healthy but flavorful food is changing restaurant cuisine, from the spa menu at The Four Seasons to the Time Cafe, an organic gourmet establishment in Greenwich Village.

• The emphasis on stress reduction and relaxation is leading to a variety of new products and services, from reflexology footwear to Ian Schrager's new urban spa at the former Barbizon Hotel in New York. Even London's indefatigable club kids are exhausted: There are "Chill Out Nights" where the "zippies" simply lie in flotariums or relax with a variety of "mind gyms," like Relaxmans—portable synchro-energizers that produce instant alpha waves via headphones. (A "zippie" as defined by Frazer Clark, editor of *Encyclopaedia Psychedelia*, "is a combination of a Sixties hippie and a Nineties technoperson.)[6]

• The interest in body/mind awareness, together with the aging of the population, is causing many people to abandon strenuous exercise, like running and high-impact aerobics, in favor of physical/mental exercise, like yoga and tai chi.

• The growing recognition of the therapeutic influence of fragrance on our emotional state can be seen in everything from upscale aromatherapy products to mass market potpourris.

• The specialty store orientation is leading to a new type of ecological store, such as the Terre Verde Trading Company in Soho or Earthsake in San Francisco, which specializes in environmentally responsible merchandise.

MARKETING AND PROMOTION

In the face of potential consumer backlash to the specious green marketing that is taking place, businesses should proceed with caution; informed Alpha consumers will immediately detect any inconsistencies in your green positioning. Alpha consumers are not alone in their skepticism: According to a 1990 study conducted by polling firm Environmental Research Associates of Princeton, New Jersey, 47 percent of consumers have come to dismiss most environmental claims as mere gimmickery.[7] A few guidelines include:

• Recognize that environmentalism is a perceived product benefit, but it is not a unique selling proposition.

EARTHSAKE IN SAN FRANCISCO
One of the leaders in the new type of ecological stores specializing in
environmentally responsible merchandise.

• Facilitate recycling opportunities. MAC—Make-Up Art
Cosmetics—for example, offers consumers one free lipstick for
every six empty containers returned.[8]

• Avoid the appearance of hypocrisy. For example, when
Bristol-Myers Squibb packages Ban deodorant in boxes marked
"Made From Recycled Paper," it is ludicrous because the carton
is totally unnecessary, as Procter & Gamble proved when it eliminated the outside carton for its Sure and Secret deodorants.

• Beware of claims like "environmentally friendly" that have
become as meaningless as "natural" or "light."

• Investigate reputable seals of approval, like Green Cross
or Green Seal.

• Do not jeopardize your integrity with misleading claims.

When General Motors, for example, promotes the company's improved exhaust systems, claiming that "since clean air became a national goal, we have substantially reduced exhaust emissions from our cars and trucks," the Alpha consumer knows that it was only because it was forced to by legislation—legislation GM spent millions of dollars fighting in Washington lobbies.[9] And when Procter & Gamble ran print ads for its disposable diapers featuring a picture of a fertile "soil enhancer" under the headline "Ninety days ago, this was a disposable diaper," the company failed to mention that the diaper's plastic lining had been removed first or that the composting process required a special municipal facility that is not available in most parts of the country.[10] Again, this type of deceptive advertising is not likely to trick the informed Alpha consumer.

• Avoid gratuitous advertising. For example, when the San Francisco clothing retailer Esprit urges consumers not to buy clothes they do not need, or the woman in the Toyota television commercial recites ecological clichés ("Waste is out. Saving, conserving, all that stuff's in"), the transparency is more likely to alienate consumers than impress them. In planning your advertising strategy, investigate media with a green orientation. MTV and Nickelodeon, for example, are both very involved in developing public service campaigns with an environmental message while publications like the *Utne Reader* and the guidebooks for the U.S. national parks (published by Pali Arts Communications in San Francisco) are likely to efficiently reach eco-aware consumers.

• Recognize the inherent environmental conflict that direct mail represents. According to the U.S. Postal Service, the production of the 63 billion pieces of third-class mail in 1990 required more than 5 million trees—catalogs alone caused the destruction of 70,000 acres of forest.[11]

• Sponsor public service programs, from recycling to consumer education. The Hard Rock Cafes in western states, for example, have established a "Save the Planet" department on their premises to encourage eco-awareness.[12] And in many states, it is possible for a company to "adopt" a lake or park.

• Develop promotional programs with a green orientation. Origins Natural Resources, for example, promotes its sensory therapy products with reflexology clinics in stores like Bergdorf Goodman, and Du Pont promotes its sportswear fabrics in the sponsorship of professional beach volleyball tournaments in California for the benefit of the Surfrider Foundation, an ecological group dedicated to the preservation of beaches.[13]

As with other techniques involved in successful Alpha target marketing, the green approach requires a long-term perspective; it will not generate an immediate increase in sales. But businesses that demonstrate a commitment to green marketing will position themselves for future growth.

CHECKLIST

The following checklist is essentially a summation of the previous marketing guidelines—a methodical device to help you identify the issues you should address as you formulate your marketing strategy.

CORPORATE/BRAND ASSESSMENT

Heritage

What is the existing equity? How can you leverage your equity to maximum advantage? If you are introducing a new business or product, what type of heritage is your brand positioning likely to foster?

Identity

Who are you? Is your identity based on your corporate name, your brand name, your distribution channel, or something else? What kind of company do you keep? Are you upscale or downscale? Are you exclusive or inclusive? Are you a leader or a follower?

Strengths/Weaknesses

What are your strengths? How can you capitalize on them? What are your weaknesses? How can you overcome them, or at least minimize their negative impact on your business? What are your greatest areas of opportunity? Long term? Short term?

Profile of your existing customer franchise

Who presently buys your product or service? What is their purchase motivation? What is the basis for their brand loyalty? How can you increase consumption among your existing users? How can you expand your customer franchise?

Perception among consumers and the trade

How do consumers, users and nonusers, regard you? Do you represent quality, value, status, or something else? Are you accessible or intimidating? What is your perception in the trade? Is your business growing or declining? Are you a winner or a loser? What type of trade support can you anticipate?

THE ALPHA CONSUMER

Purchase motivation in your industry

What does this consumer respond to? How does his or her purchase motivation differ from his or her mainstream counterpart?

Compatibility with your identity

Does your identity correspond to Alpha consumers' values? If not, how can you bring their values into the marketplace? If the Alpha consumer's values are incompatible with your identity, how can you monitor this influential consumer to help you identify future market opportunities?

Role in your business as users and influentials

If the Alpha consumers are users, how do you retain their brand loyalty? If they are not users, what must you do to enhance your appeal to them? What are the dynamics of your business? How do Alphas influence other consumers?

STATE OF YOUR INDUSTRY

Market trends

Is your market growing, stagnant, or declining? What future developments should you anticipate? Among consumers? Among the trade?

Competitive environment

What is driving your industry? Is it increased consumption, new users, new products, new distribution channels, promotion, or something else? How can you preempt your competitors? How can you position yourself above the competitive fray?

Government regulation

What type of government and trade regulation should you anticipate? How can you assume a progressive rather than a defensive posture?

STRATEGIC PLANNING

Areas of opportunities

What are your areas of opportunity? Do they include product improvement, line extensions, new products, new distribution, acquisitions, joint ventures, or something else? How can you utilize the Alpha consumer for directional market research to help you identify new business opportunities?

Objectives

What do you want to accomplish? Long term? Short term? What are your priorities? How can the Alpha consumer help you achieve your objectives?

Strategies

What are your alternatives? For each strategy, what is the upside potential? What is the risk? What type of competitive offensive/ defensive should you anticipate? What is your contingency plan? Should you target Alpha consumers with a niche marketing approach or develop a broad-based plan that will incorporate the Alpha consumer?

Resources required, both financial and managerial

To successfully execute your strategy and accomplish your objectives, what type of financial resources are required? How much do you need to invest in research and development, operations, and marketing to maximize profitability? Do you have the personnel necessary to execute your strategy? Do you need to recruit new talent?

MARKETING

Product positioning

What is your differential advantage? What makes your business unique? What perceived benefits does your product offer the Alpha consumer? The mainstream consumer?

Product development

How can you incorporate the Alpha consumer into your product development process? What role should broad-based consumer research play? Where should you look for new directions? Do you need to go outside of your standard product development channels?

Pricing

What is your product or service worth to the Alpha consumer? Does it represent quality, value, cachet, or something else? How much price elasticity exists in your industry? Where do you want to be vis-à-vis your competitors? Should you introduce a product at a premium price-point to establish cachet and then take minimum price increases in the face of competitive increases, enabling you to maintain your cachet while representing growing value to the consumer? Should you discount?

Distribution/Location

Which distribution channels or locations will maximize the appeal of your business to the Alpha consumer? Should you emphasize convenience, mystique, or something else? If you do not have your own distribution channels, how can you still maximize control of your business?

Customer service

What type of statement do you want to make? What services should you provide? What type of people should represent you to consumers? Should you emphasize expertise, image, or something else? How can you hire, train, and motivate appropriate customer service personnel?

Direct marketing

What is the potential of direct marketing in your business? Should you invest in direct mail, a toll-free number, or home delivery? How can you develop an Alpha mailing list? What incentive can you provide the Alpha consumer?

Public relations

How do you generate a buzz among Alpha consumers? What is your greatest public relations resource? Is it your product, your personnel, your philanthropy, your customers, or something else? How do you identify the media most likely to influence the Alpha consumer?

Advertising

Should you advertise? Do you want to create an insider's cachet for your business among Alpha consumers or achieve mainstream brand awareness? What is your primary advertising objective? Is it creating awareness, maintaining awareness, image enhancement, promotional, or something else? Do you have news or information to convey to the Alpha consumer that is likely to motivate purchase?

Promotion

Should you assume a promotional posture? What is the impact of sampling or trial, frequency programs, special offers, special events, cross-promotions and tie-ins, price promotions, coupons, premiums, contests, and sweepstakes on the Alpha consumer? On the mainstream? What are the advantages of promotion? What are the risks?

To ensure an integrated marketing strategy, once you have completed the checklist, go back and randomly cross-reference various elements for consistency, the type of consistency that will create a distinctive brand identity. If there is no logical correspondence, you should probably rethink your strategy.

CLOSING THOUGHTS

In targeting the trendsetting consumer, every business must develop a strategy that is appropriate for its industry, its heritage or brand identity, and its marketing objectives. We have attempted to formulate some general marketing guidelines, but every business is unique and should be approached on an individual basis. In closing, we would like to remind you that targeted Alpha marketing frequently requires a long-term perspective. Due to their limited numbers, Alpha consumers alone are unlikely to generate immediate sales increases. However, the endorsement of the Alpha consumer over time may be the key to establishing—and maintaining—a desirable brand identity in the eyes of the mainstream, which will enable you to achieve long-term profitability. In targeting the Alpha consumer, remember that everything you do sends a distinct message to this discerning customer; superior quality, a clear brand identity, consistency, and a fanatical attention to detail will be noticed and appreciated—and be the foundation for brand loyalty.

NOTES

CHAPTER 2: WHY ARE THEY IMPORTANT?

1. A. Ramirez, "Revlon Deal Would Realign Industry," *New York Times*, March 5, 1991, p. D6.

CHAPTER 3: PURCHASE BEHAVIOR

1. J. Walls, "Bendel's Debuts Without a Bendel," *New York Magazine*, March 18, 1991, p. 10.

CHAPTER 4: MONITORING THE TRENDSETTING CONSUMER

1. A. Fahey, "H20 Marketers Mop Damage," *Advertising Age*, April 15, 1991, p. 1.
2. G. Levin, "Cutler: Planning in an Uncertain Market," *Advertising Age*, February 11, 1991, p. 4.
3. S. Shamoon, "Adweek Diary," *Adweek*, February 4, 1991, p. 8.
4. Dennis Thim, "Lagerfeld's Animal Kingdom," *Women's Wear Daily*, July 27, 1990, p. 7.
5. Eye, "Gaultier Takes New York," *Women's Wear Daily*, April 16, 1991, p. 24.
6. N. Darnton, "Fashion: The Ultimate Squeeze Play," *Newsweek*, May 13, 1991, p. 63.
7. F. A. Bernstein, "For Ian Schrager, Design Is Paramount," *Metropolitan Home*, November 1990, p. 63.

8. G. Wayne, "In Search of the Tastemakers," *Paper*, November 1990, p. 18.

9. G. Wayne, ibid.

10. C. Gandee, "Ian Schrager Is the Host of the Town," *HG*, October 1990, p. 260.

11. W. Norwich, "Ian Goes Solo," *Vanity Fair*, August 1990, p. 115.

12. G. Wayne, "In the Raw," *Paper*, November 1990.

13. R. La Ferla, "Cool Customers," *New York Times Magazine*, June 30, 1991, p. 24.

14. B. Svetkey, "Retail's Art and Kraft Movement," *Adweek*, April 2, 1990, p. 26.

CHAPTER 5: LONG-TERM SUCCESSES

1. M. Magiera, "Levi's Boosts Ads," *Advertising Age*, April 15, 1991, p. 17.

2. A.-M. Schiro, "All About Denim," *New York Times*, February 3, 1991, p. F4.

3. Corporate Strategies, "Levi Strauss: A Touch of Fashion—and Humility," *Business Week*, October 24, 1983, p. 85.

4. Vogue's View, "Shopping L.A.," *Vogue*, May 1991, p. 128.

5. K. Fitzgerald, "People: Kathleen Demitros," *Advertising Age*, January 8, 1990, p. 32.

6. R. L. Rose, "Vrooming Back: After Nearly Stalling, Harley-Davidson Finds New Crowd of Riders," *Wall Street Journal*, August 31, 1990, p. A1.

7. C. Singer, "After Buying Back The Firm, Harley-Davidson's New Execs Take Their Act On The Road," *People*, July 13, 1981, p. 32.

8. C. Singer, ibid.

9. C. Singer, ibid.

10. Follow Through, "Harley's Hogs," *Forbes*, December 2, 1985, p. 14.

11. L. Bird, "Butch Cassidy and the Cluttered Charge Card Market," *Adweek's Marketing Week*, December 18, 1989, p. 6.

12. J. McManus and Alison Fahey, "AmEx Works Weekends," *Advertising Age*, October 15, 1990, p. 2.

13. L. Castro, "Optima Tries to Expand Base in Test Market," *Wall Street Journal*, December 17, 1990, p. B1.

14. M. Lewis, "Leave Home Without It," *The New Republic*, September 4, 1989, p. 19.

15. A. Chambers, "Author Stephen King's Spooky AmEx Commercial

Caps A Decade of 'Do You Know Me's?'," *People*, August 27, 1984, p. 96.

16. P. Patton, "Why Sony Is Betting So Big on Such a Small Format," *Adweek's Marketing Week*, February 12, 1990, p. 20.

17. K. Deveny, "Electronics Makers Are Wooing Women After Years of Taking Them For Granted," *Wall Street Journal*, December 28, 1990, p. 9.

CHAPTER 6: EVOLUTIONARY SUCCESSES

1. A. M. Freedman, "Perrier Finds Mystique Hard to Restore," *Wall Street Journal*, December 2, 1990, p. B1.

2. M. Hochstein, "New Brands Rush to Battle in Perrier Water Market," *Nation's Restaurant News*, February 11, 1991.

3. J. Reitman, "Club Med's New 'Antidote' Mixes Fun, Families, and Business," *Marketing & Media Decisions*, Spring 1985 Special, p. 51.

4. "Company Brief: Club Med," *The Economist*, July 12, 1986, p. 78.

5. J. Levine, "I Am Sorry, We Have Changed," *Forbes*, September 4, 1989, p. 136.

6. L. Robinson, "Rock Talk: We Still Want Our MTV," *New York Post*, June 21, 1989, p. 25.

7. S. Heller Anderson, "Celebrating Mirabella's 2nd Anniversary," *New York Times*, June 28, 1991, p. B6.

8. M. Winkleman, "Magazine World 1991," *Adweek*, February 18, 1991, p. M.25.

CHAPTER 7: REPOSITIONING SUCCESSES

1. W.Hochswender, "Patterns: An Active Weekend," *New York Times*, March 5, 1991, p. B7.

2. "On Target," *Women's Wear Daily*, June 4, 1991, p. 4.

3. G. Howell, "Royalist Leanings," *Vogue*, April 1989, p. 381.

4. G. Howell, ibid.

5. N. Darnton, "Multiple Choices," *Newsweek*, November 5, 1990, p. 68.

6. N. Darnton, ibid.

7. B. Morris, "At Chanel and Dior, New Vigor," *New York Times*, October 23, 1990, p. B8.

8. "Chanel Plumps Up Its Lashes," *Women's Wear Daily*, March 1, 1991, p. 13.
9. D. Wood, "Chanel's Égöiste: Bottling the Myth," *Women's Wear Daily*, February 22, 1991, p. 18.
10. MPA ad, "Marketing Success Stories," *Adweek*, March 4, 1991, p. 26.
11. MPA ad, ibid.
12. B. Bagot, "Neat Shot," *Marketing & Media Decisions*, March 1989, p. 73.
13. S. Feinberg, "Customers Avoid Stores' Game of Markup/Markdown," *Women's Wear Daily*, August 22, 1990, p. 9.
14. F. Schwadel, "Going Without: Gap Drops Anchors in Its Plan to Develop Upscale Malls," *Wall Street Journal*, October 25, 1990, p. B1.
15. B. Kantrowitz, "Now You Can Crawl into the Gap," *Newsweek*, October 29, 1990, p. 86.
16. S. Feinberg, "The Gap's Formula for Success," *Women's Wear Daily*, August 24, 1990, p. 9.
17. S. Feinberg, ibid.
18. F. Schwadel, "At Gap, Clothes Make the Ads as Stars Fade," *Wall Street Journal*, December 3, 1990, p. B6.
19. I. Barmash, "Gap Finds Middle Road to Success," *New York Times*, June 24, 1991, p. D1.
20. W. Hochswender, "It's Glam! It's Fab! It's a Rave!," *New York Times*, December 2, 1990, p. F1.
21. I. Barmash, "Japanese Back New Barneys Store," *New York Times*, November 16, 1990, p. D1.
22. I. Barmash, ibid.
23. M. Merris, "Barneys New York Is Going Uptown," *Women's Wear Daily*, November 16, 1990, p. 5.
24. B. Bagot, ibid.

CHAPTER 9: TOO-SOON-TO-TELL SUCCESSES

1. C. Madison, "Blade Maneuvers to Stay on a Roll," *Adweek*, March 4, 1991, p. 20.
2. T. Murray, "The Wind at Nike's Back," *Adweek's Marketing Week*, November 14, 1988, p. 28.
3. C. Madison, ibid.
4. M. Magiera, "Nike Takes Global Steps," *Advertising Age*, January 14, 1991, p. 3.

5. "100 Leading Advertisers," *Advertising Age*, September 26, 1990, p. 97.
6. G. Eskenazi, "Once a Canvas Shoe, Now a Big-Time Player," *New York Times*, March 11, 1990, p. 26.
7. G. Eskenazi, ibid.
8. M. Grimm, "The Sneaker Brands Lose Their Bounce," *Adweek's Marketing Week*, January 7, 1991, p. 9.
9. R. Fannin, "Mazda's Sporting Chance," *Marketing and Media Decisions*, October 1989, p. 24.
10. D. Kiley, "Mazda Prepares to Give Honda, Toyota a Run for Their Money," *Adweek's Marketing Week*, August 8, 1988, p. 25.
11. D. P. Levin, "Hot Wheels," *New York Times Magazine*, September 30, 1990, p. 32.
12. R. Fannin, ibid.
13. R. Fannin, ibid.
14. D. P. Levin, ibid.
15. D. Kiley, "Rod Bymaster," *Adweek's Marketing Week*, November 27, 1989, p. M.R.C. 29.
16. "Body Shop Lowers U.S. Losses," *Women's Wear Daily*, June 5, 1991, p. 2.
17. P. Street, "Body Shop: Stretching Out," *Women's Wear Daily*, December 18, 1990, p. 10.
18. T. Clifton, "Cosmetics With a Conscience," *Newsweek*, February 12, 1990, p. 65.
19. T. Clifton, ibid.
20. P. Street, ibid.
21. T. Clifton, ibid.
22. T. Clifton, ibid.

CHAPTER 10: SHORT-TERM SUCCESSES

1. K. Deveny, "Reality of the '90's Hits Yuppie Brands," *Wall Street Journal*, December 20, 1990, p. B1.
2. C. Madison, "Blade Maneuvers to Stay on a Roll," *Advertising Age*, March 4, 1991, p. 20.
3. J. Dornberg, "Up From Swatch," *Business Month*, March 1988, p. 57.
4. R. Shriner, *Marketing To Kids Report*, (April 1990, Volume 3, No. 7.)
5. E. Diamond, "Media: Puck's Bad Boys," *New York*, July 27, 1987, p. 16.

6. J. Walls, "Intelligencer: Spy Comes in From the Cold," *New York*, March 18, 1991, p. 9.

7. I. Cohen Selinger and K. McCormack, "Spy-ing on Saatchi and Ex-CEOs," *Adweek*, January 1, 1991, p. 2.

8. Selinger and McCormack, ibid.

9. Selinger and McCormack, ibid.

10. C. Sandler, "The Pursuit of Trivia Dollars," *Publishers Weekly*, February 15, 1985, p. 74.

11. J. P. Tarpey, "Selchow & Righter: Playing Trivial Pursuit to the Limit," *Business Week*, November 26, 1984.

12. J. P. Tarpey, ibid.

13. A. Leigh Cowan, "A Game Maker's Winning Moves," *New York Times*, July 4, 1991, p. D1.

CHAPTER 11: MISSED OPPORTUNITIES

1. P. Sloan, "Avon Is Calling on New Tactics, FCB," *Advertising Age*, January 7, 1991, p. 3.

2. J. Phillips, *You'll Never Eat Lunch in This Town Again*, (New York: Random House, 1991), p. 18.

3. A. B. Longley, "Crystal Brands—Company Report," Donaldson, Lufkin, Jenrette, Inc., October 2, 1990, p. 5.

4. B. Saporito, "When Business Got So Good, It Got Dangerous," *Fortune*, April 2, 1984, p. 61.

5. B. Saporito, ibid.

6. B. Gall, "Crystal Brands—Company Report," Merrill Lynch, October 16, 1990, p. 1.

CHAPTER 12: STRATEGIC PLANNING

1. L. Savan, "Sneakers and Nothingness," *Village Voice*, April 2, 1991, p. 43.

2. C. Heimel, "Trends: Where Are They?," *Voice*, January 22, 1991, p. 44.

3. E. Smith, "It's Anyone's Guess," *Mediaweek*, February 11, 1991, p. 26.

4. K. Deveny, "Perelman's Vaunted Marketing Skills Produce Only Mixed Results at Revlon," *Wall Street Journal*, March 4, 1991, p. B1.

5. J. Dagnoli, "Beware Line Extensions," *Advertising Age*, October 29, 1990, p. 52.
6. B. Kanner, "On Madison Avenue: Going, Going, Gone," *New York*, February 18, 1991, p. 19.
7. B. Kanner, ibid.
8. J. Dagnoli, ibid.
9. P. Green, "Beauty: The Sweet Smell of Excess," *New York Times Magazine*, February 10, 1991, p. 52.
10. B. Saporito, "Companies That Compete Best," *Fortune*, May 22, 1989, p. 36.
11. N. Gross and W. J. Holstein, "Why Sony Is Plugging Into Columbia," *Business Week*, October 16, 1989, p. 56.
12. J. Huey, "America's Hottest Export: Pop Culture," *Fortune*, December 31, 1990, p. 50.
13. "Puck's Ploy—Exciting Food, Fresh Beer," *National Restaurant News*, August 13, 1990, p. 20.
14. R. Rothenberg, "If It Gallops or Waltzes, License It," *New York Times*, June 20, 1991, p. D1.
15. R. Rothenberg, ibid.
16. J. Huey, ibid.

CHAPTER 13: SEMIOTICS

1. "Revitalizing the Image of Hearst," *Advertising Age*, February 8, 1991, p. 20.
2. R. Crain, "Brand Building on the Rebound," *Advertising Age*, March 18, 1991, p. 34.
3. J. Grierson, "Trendy Restaurants Work Hard Shooting for the Hip," *Wall Street Journal*, August 28, 1990, p. B2.
4. J. B. Hinge, "Critics Call Cuts in Package Size Deceptive Move," *Wall Street Journal*, February 5, 1991, p. B1.

CHAPTER 14: VISUAL DESIGN

1. R. La Ferla, "Men's Style: Be A Sport," *New York Times Magazine*, November 18, 1990, p. 78.
2. S. Slesin, "Reality Strikes Milan Like a Flashback," *New York Times*, April 18, 1991, p. C1.
3. M. Gordon, "Demob's Message: Entertaining Shoppers," *Women's Wear Daily*, October 3, 1990, p. 18.

4. L. Wells, "Boutique Chic," *New York Times Magazine*, February 19, 1989, p. 60.

CHAPTER 15: DISTRIBUTION AND LOCATION

1. J. Holusha, "How Harley Outfoxed Japan With Exports," *New York Times*, August 12, 1990, p. F5.
2. B. Kanner, "On Madison Avenue: When You're Haute You're Hot," *New York*, January 27, 1986, p. 14.
3. B. Kanner, ibid.
4. "Lacroix Scent Cuts Back Its Distribution in U.S." *Women's Wear Daily*, January 21, 1991, p. 15.
5. J. Grierson, "Trendy Restaurants Work Hard Shooting for the Hip," *Wall Street Journal*, August 28, 1990, p. B2.
6. L. Brody, "Name That Street," *Los Angeles*, November 1990, p. 22.

CHAPTER 16: CUSTOMER SERVICE

1. S. Feinberg, "Retailing Today: Specialty Stores in Forefront," *Women's Wear Daily*, September 5, 1990, p. 16.
2. I. Barmash, "Bloomingdale's Is Closing Store in Queens, Its First Branch," *New York Times*, May 2, 1991, p. B4.
3. D. Vreeland, *D.V.* (New York: Alfred A. Knopf, 1984), p. 135.
4. A. Ward, "The Gap Opens the Door to New Mall Concepts," *Advertising Age*, January 21, 1991, p. 39.
5. J. Kron, "The Image Police," *Allure*, March 1991, p. 96.
6. J. Kron, ibid.
7. A. Stille, "A Degree From Disneyworld," *New York Times*, January 13, 1991, p. 35.
8. D. Kleiman, "Retro Magnate Moves East," *New York Times*, February 13, 1991, p. C1.
9. L. Shapiro, "Table for Everyone," *Newsweek*, July 8, 1991, p. 64.
10. S. L. Hwang, "Marketing," *Wall Street Journal*, March 4, 1991, p. B1.
11. R. Powell, "It's One Party Even the Recession Can't Spoil," *New York Times*, June 23, 1991, p. 10F.
12. J. Kron, ibid.
13. C. Gandee, "Ian Schrager Is the Host of the Town," *HG*, October 1990, p. 260.

CHAPTER 17: DIRECT MARKETING

1. "Business: Pages and Pages of Pain," *Newsweek*, May 27, 1991, p. 39.
2. L. Williams, "Consumers vs Callers: The Lines Are Busier," *New York Times*, June 20, 1991, p. C1.
3. J. Schwartz, "How Did They Get My Name?", *Newsweek*, June 3, 1991, p. 40.
4. L. Lockwood, "Sportswear Report," *Women's Wear Daily*, February 6, 1991, p. 10.
5. M. Miller, " 'Greens' Add to Junk Mail Mountain," *Wall Street Journal*, May 13, 1991, p. B1.
6. E. Newhall, "The Art of the Appeal," *New York*, February 18, 1991, p. 29.
7. D. Hofman, "Shopping in Europe From Home," *New York Times*, May 4, 1991, p. 48.
8. N. R. Kleinfield, "Even for J. Crew, the Mail-Order Boom Days Are Over," *New York Times*, September 2, 1990, p. F5.
9. F. Rice, "How to Deal With Tougher Customers," *Fortune*, December 3, 1990, p. 39.
10. K. Kerr, "Where Should Advertising Be?," *Adweek's Marketing Week*, May 6, 1991, p. 26.
11. F. Rice, ibid.
12. F. Rice, ibid.
13. F. Warner, "Surprise! Chiquita Advises: Eat Bananas," *Adweek's Marketing Week*, April 29, 1991, p. 8.

CHAPTER 18: PUBLIC RELATIONS

1. G. Doppelt, "Talking Fashion," *Vogue*, July 1989, p. 217.
2. P. M. Reilly, "Daring Debutante: Condé Nast's Allure," *Wall Street Journal*, December 21, 1990, p. B1.
3. R. Turner, "Disney's Star Is Foreign to U.S. Audiences," *Wall Street Journal*, December 21, 1990, p. B1.
4. J. Pereira, "Name of the Game: Brand Awareness," *Wall Street Journal*, February 14, 1991, p. B1.
5. W. Norwich, "Ian Goes Solo," *Vanity Fair*, August 1990, p. 115.
6. F. A. Bernstein, "For Ian Schrager, Design Is Paramount," *Metropolitan Home*, November 1990, p. 63.
7. J. Wolfe, "All About Nancy," *Advertising Age*, April 15, 1991, p. 50.

8. R. Cohen, "Nancy Reagan Followers," *New York Times*, July 3, 1991, p. C17.

9. G. Greene, "The Insatiable Critic: Bon Jour et Nuit," *New York*, November 19, 1990, p. 74.

10. G. Greene, ibid.

11. J. Grierson, "Trendy Restaurants Work Hard Shooting for the Hip," *Wall Street Journal*, August 28, 1990, p. B2.

12. K. Springen and A. Miller, "Business: Doing the Right Thing," *Newsweek*, January 7, 1991, p. 42.

13. L. Bird, "Event Marketing: Seagram Takes to the Stage," *Adweek's Marketing Week*, January 7, 1991, p. 17.

14. N. Salik, *The Marketing to Kids Report*, (April 1990, Volume 3, No. 7).

15. R. Rothenberg, "Critics Seek F.T.C. Action on Products as Movie Stars," *New York Times*, May 31, 1991, p. D1.

CHAPTER 19: ADVERTISING

1. J. Steinhauer, "Turnaround Time at Ogilvy," *New York Times*, April 2, 1991, p. F10.

2. J. Liesse, "How the Bunny Changed Eveready," *Advertising Age*, April 8, 1991, p. 20.

3. J. Bartimo, "PC Survey Winner From J.D. Power Has Cause to Crow," *Wall Street Journal*, May 14, 1991, p. B6.

4. K. Jacobsen, "David Ogilvy," *Adweek*, January 28, 1991, p. 16.

5. S. Elliott, "Wieden's Hope: Victory Will Build Its Creative Name," *New York Times*, June 24, 1991, p. D6.

6. J. Lafayette, "Buckley, Decerchio try California," *Advertising Age*, May 6, 1991, p. 22.

7. E. de Bono, "Advertising People Aren't Creative," *Advertising Age*, December 3, 1990, p. 30.

8. J. Kurtzman, "Disloyal American Buyers Are Detroit's Latest Challenge," *New York Times*, June 23, 1991, p. F2.

9. J. Lipman, "Ads on TV: Out of Sight, Out of Mind?", *Wall Street Journal*, May 14, 1991, p. B1.

10. M. J. McCarthy, "Mind Probe," *Wall Street Journal*, March 22, 1991, p. B3.

11. P. Stevenson, "Ed McCabe," *Details*, May 1991, p. 81.

12. A. L. Stern, "Converse in Adland, Playing Catch-Up Ball," *New York Times*, March 24, 1991, p. F5.

13. M. Lev, "Leo Burnett Makes the Case for the Comparative Method," *New York Times*, April 23, 1991, p. D22.
14. P. Winters, "Diet Colas Drop Comparative Tactic," *Advertising Age*, January 21, 1991, p. 24.
15. P. Winters, ibid.
16. L. Bird, "Butch Cassidy and the Cluttered Charge Card Market," *Adweek's Marketing Week*, December 18, 1989, p. 6.
17. B. Lippert, "L'Oréal Puts Intelligent Face on Makeup Ad," *Adweek*, May 13, 1991, p. 16.
18. M. Gross, "Star Bores," *New York*, April 29, 1991, p. 32.
19. M. Gross, ibid.
20. "Elements of Style: Why I Wear What I Wear," *GQ*, November 1990, p. 98.
21. D. Kiley, "Isuzu Quits Its Lying Ways and Gives Della Femina the Boot," *Adweek's Marketing Week*, May 13, 1991, p. 6.
22. B. Garfield, "Familiar Faces Put New Fizz in Familiar Idea for A & W Soda," *Advertising Age*, January 14, 1991, p. 46.
23. J. S. Lubin, "Magazines Helping Advertisers Measure Response to Their Ads," *Wall Street Journal*, January 16, 1991, p. B5.
24. "Brown: Aping TV a Blunder," *Advertising Age*, May 13, 1991, p. 48.

CHAPTER 20: PROMOTION

1. B. Hulin-Salkin, "Demise of the Discount," *Incentive*, September 1990, p. 27.
2. B. Hulin-Salkin, ibid.
3. R. Alsop, "Brand Loyalty Is Rarely Blind Loyalty," *Wall Street Journal*, October 19, 1989, p. B1.
4. B. Hulin-Sakin, ibid.
5. J. E. Rigdon, "Kodak Zooms In on Pro Photographers," *Wall Street Journal*, February 27, 1991, p. B1.
6. P. Frumkin, "Instinct, Imagination: Pino Luongo's Ingredients for Success," *Nation's Restaurant News*, February 18, 1991, p. 25.
7. E. Penzer, "Measuring Special Events," *Incentive*, October 1990, p. 162.
8. T. R. King, "Advertising: Thus Far, Bacardi Breezers Look Like the Wine Coolers of the '90s," *Wall Street Journal*, April 18, 1991, p. B4.
9. J. Pereira, "Name of the Game: Brand Awareness," *Wall Street Journal*, February 14, 1991, p. B1.

10. C. Fisher, "Wal-Mart's Way," *Advertising Age*, February 18, 1991, p. 3.
11. I. Barmash, "Brooks Brothers Stays the Course," *New York Times*, November 23, 1990, p. D1.
12. P. C. T. Elsworth, "Can Colors and Stripes Rescue Shirt Makers From a Slump?" *New York Times*, March 17, 1991, p. F5.
13. *Women's Wear Daily*, March 1, 1991, p. 6.
14. Bloomingdale's ad, *New York Times*, February 10, 1991, p. B5.
15. L. Peterson, "Flying Taters for an FSI Is a Half-Baked Idea," *Adweek*, February 4, 1991, p. 21.
16. S. W. Phillips, "PR's Place in the Marketing Mix," *Food & Beverage Marketing*, July 1990, p. 10.
17. A. Fahy, "Pepsi, Coke Tune into Summer Fun," *Advertising Age*, May 13, 1991, p. 3.
18. M. Magiera, "Hitchcock on Air for Nickelodeon," *Advertising Age*, October 29, 1990, p. 12.

CHAPTER 21: GREEN MARKETING

1. J. Motavalli, "Selling Guilt-Free Consumerism," *Adweek*, August 1, 1988, p. M.R.C. 4.
2. J. Motavalli, ibid.
3. J. Schwartz, "It's Not Easy Being Green," *Newsweek*, November 19, 1990, p. 51.
4. "Americans Are Happy Campers," *New York Times*, May 19, 1991, section 5, p. 3.
5. F. Fabricant, "Yesterday's Favorite Cleansers Make Modern Homes Gleam," *New York Times*, February 14, 1991, p. C12.
6. E. Nickson, "Zip Up," *US*, November 12, 1990, p. 17.
7. J. Schwartz, ibid.
8. C. Smith, "MAC Attack," *New York*, June 3, 1991, p. 22.
9. E. Penzer, "Turning Green," *Incentive*, July 1990, p. 26.
10. M. Green, "Recyclable . . . or Just Fraudulents?", *New York Times*, April 21, 1991, p. F11.
11. M. Miller, " 'Greens' Add to Junk Mail Mountain," *Wall Street Journal*, May 13, 1991, p. B1.
12. R. Martin, "Hard Rock Cafes Take Stand on Environmental Concerns," *Restaurant News*, February 19, 1990.
13. "Havland on the Half Shell," *Sportstyle*, October 22, 1990.

INDEX

A

ABC, 153
Abdul, Paula, 164
Absolut Vodka, 21, 37, 43, 62, 65–67, 71, 89, 119, 152, 155, 157, 161, 162, 169, 171–72, 175
A. C. Neilsen, 177
Adidas, 78
Advertising, ix, viii, 1, 11, 15, 17, 18, 20, 21, 22, 25, 26, 28, 29, 30, 31, 34–35, 37, 39, 42, 43, 46, 49, 51, 53, 54, 58, 59, 62–63, 64, 65–66, 68–69, 71, 72, 73, 74, 76–77, 78, 79, 83, 85, 86, 87, 89, 100, 101, 104, 105, 106, 112, 113, 126–27, 141, 143, 144, 147, 151, 155–68, 170, 180, 184, 192
Advertising Age, 36, 42, 81, 113, 143, 167
Adweek, 165
Adweek's Marketing Week, 141
AIDS, 71, 72, 150, 151, 176
Allure, 144
Altchuler, Murray, 110
Always, 81
AMC Movie Theaters, 134
American Association of Advertising Agencies, 159
American Express Co., 18, 35, 43, 48–51, 53–54, 104, 126, 162, 164
Americo, Jo-Jo, 34
Ann Taylor, 67
Apple Computer Company, 119
Aqua Net Hairspray, 44, 73, 74
Aramis, 10, 108
Arbus, Doon, 21
Architectural Digest, 30
Arm & Hammer Baking Soda, 181
Armani, Giorgio. *See* Emporio Armani; Giorgio Armani
Aromatherapy, 25, 32, 182
The Arts, 6, 7, 8, 35, 65–66, 112, 132, 134, 146, 151, 152
Astor, Brooke, 47
Astor Place Barber Shop, 4
Asuag-SSIH, 88
Atlas, Jeffrey, 69
Atlas Citron Haligman & Bedecarre, 69

Automobiles, 29, 30, 35, 42, 44, 56, 75, 77, 80–82, 85, 105, 116, 117, 121, 143, 151, 155, 158, 160, 167, 184
Aveda Corporation, 8
Avedon, Burt Simm, 117
Avedon, Richard, 21
"The Avengers," 81
Avon Products, 44, 92, 93, 97, 109
A Votre Sante Restaurant, 130

B

"Babe" Brandelli's Brig, 130
Bacall, Lauren, 164
Bacardi Imports, 174
Bahrenburg, D. Claeys, 112
Bakker, Tammy Faye, 71
Baldwin, Alec, 136
Ban Deodorant, 183
Bang and Olufson, 117
Barbarella, 30
Barbizon Hotel, 33, 182
Barkin, Ellen, 143
Barnes, Jake, 158
Barneys New York, 6, 34–35, 43, 62, 63, 69–72, 104, 119, 122, 145, 152, 155
Barr, Roseanne, 153
Barton Beers Ltd., 86, 87, 91
Bartsch, Suzanne, 71, 72
Basile, Andy, 63
Basinger, Kim, 68
Bausch and Lomb, 154
bbc, 105, 123, 136, 143
BBDO, 164
Beals, Vaughn, 47, 48, 104
Beard, James, 143
The Beatles, 35
Beef Industry Council, 164
Beene, Geoffrey. *See* Geoffrey Beene
Ben & Jerry's Ice Cream, 22, 44, 75, 76, 77, 79–80, 85, 104, 130, 150, 151, 155, 169, 180
Bendel, Henri, 20
Benetton, 163
Bergdorf Goodman, 5, 11, 63, 70, 111, 122, 185
Bernhard, Sandra, 143

Berstein, Fred A., 41
Betsy Johnson, 39, 41
Bettina Riedel, 138
Beverages, 17, 18, 21, 26, 34, 37, 39, 40, 43, 44,
    55–56, 60–61, 62, 65–67, 71, 73, 74, 86–87,
    89, 91, 108–10, 116, 117, 119, 121, 122, 126,
    143, 152, 155, 156, 157, 160, 161, 162, 164–
    65, 166–67, 169, 171–72, 174, 175, 177, 178
Beyond, Billy, 145
Biel, Alex, 162
Billboard, 36
Black, Joanne, 50
Blackglama Mink, 31, 162
Blass, Bill, 51
Block, Judith, 134
Bloomingdale, Betsy, 89
Bloomingdale's, 26, 37, 93, 94, 121, 131, 176
BMW, 56, 82
The Body Shop, 44, 75, 77, 83–84, 85, 104,
    116, 122, 123, 123, 128, 130, 140, 150, 155,
    180
Bond, James, 81–82, 154
Bonfire of the Vanities, 30
Bowie, David, 114, 165
BP Reports, 148
Bracher, Judy, 138
Brady, James, 143
"The Brady Bunch," 39
Brando, Marlon, 46, 47
Breezers, 174
Breuer, Marcel, 16
Brick, Chris, 105, 123, 136, 143
Bristol-Myers Squibb, 183
The Broadway, 125
Brooks Brothers, 166, 176
Brown, Helen Gurley, 144
Brown, Tina, 22, 145, 168
Brubach, Holly, 42
Bruce, Evangeline, 144
Buckley/DeCerchio/Cavalier, 159
Budweiser Beer, 44, 73, 74
Bymaster, Rod, 81

C

Cafe Luxembourg, 149
Caldwell, Sarah, 51
Calvin Klein. *See* Klein, Calvin
Calvin Klein Cosmetic Corporation, 171
Cameron, Kirk, 164
Campbell-Mithun-Esty, 75, 87
Canal Bar, 149
Canon Photura Camera, 121
Capri Restaurant, 130
Carillon Importers, 62–63, 66, 104
Carmex Inc., 180
Cartier, 176
Carver, Raymond, 143
CBGB, 94
CBS, 168
CBS Records, 109
Celebration, 143
Celestial Seasonings, 122

Chamberlain, Wilt, 49
Chanel, viii, 43, 62, 63–65, 70–71, 104, 105,
    106, 108, 116, 117, 119, 121, 123, 126, 128,
    135, 139, 148–49, 169
Channeling, 179
Charles, Ray, 164
Chateau Marmont Hotel, 41, 122, 143
Chateau Mouton-Rothschild, 37
Chemical Bank, 178
Cher, 39
Chevrolet, 160
Chiat, Jay, 112
Chiat/Day/Mojo, 112, 162
Chinois Restaurant, 22
Chiquita Brands, 142
Chopin, 135
Christian Lacroix, 127, 147
Chrysler Corporation, 29, 158
Clarins, 121
Clark, Frazer, 182
Clemente, Francesco, 71
Click, 42
Clinique, 10, 108, 139, 177–78
Clio Awards, 68
Club Med, 43, 56–57, 60–61, 114
"Club MTV," 59
CNN, 35, 36
Coca-Cola, 18, 21, 156, 164–65, 178
Coffee Shop Restaurant, 113
Cohen, Ben, 22, 76, 79–80, 150
Coleman, Jay, 165
Columbia Pictures, 109
Comme Des Garcons, 143
Commercial Break, 165
Condé Nast, 60, 144, 145
Confetti, 122
Connick, Harry, Jr., 4
Connoisseur, 112
Continental Airlines, 174
Converse, 78, 163
Coors Beer, 26
Corona Beer, 26, 44, 86–87, 91
Corporate Philanthropy, 12, 15, 19, 66, 72, 79–
    80, 101, 146
Cosmair Inc., 16, 22, 165
Cosmetics, viii, 5, 10–11, 16, 18, 21, 22, 35, 39,
    43, 44, 59, 62, 63–65, 70–71, 73, 74, 75, 77,
    83–84, 85, 92, 93, 95–96, 97, 104, 105, 106,
    107, 108, 109, 116, 117, 119, 121, 122, 123,
    126, 128, 130, 135, 139, 140, 143, 145, 148–
    49, 150, 155, 158, 160, 163, 165, 167, 169,
    171, 177–78, 180, 181, 183, 184–85
Cosmopolitan, 144
Costello, Dick, 161
Costner, Kevin, 46
Courreges, 37
Crain, Rance, 113
Cruise, Tom, 46, 154
Cry Baby, 37
Crystal, Billy, 164
Crystal Brands, 97
Crystals, 179
Cuervo Gold, 174

Currie, Alannah, 88
Customer Service, ix, 24, 68, 71, 72, 100, 112, 131–36, 141, 191
Cutler, Laurel, 29

D

D'Arcy Masius Benton & Bowles, 170
Davidson, William, 48
Dean, James, 46
Dean & Deluca, 123, 147
de Bono, Edward, 159
DeCerchio, Tom, 159, 160
Deeee-lite, 39
de la Renta, Annette, 46–47
Demitros, Kathleen, 47
Demob, 105
Depardieu, Gerard, 146
Depp, Johnny, 37
Design. *See* Interior Design; Visual Design
Details, 37, 41, 106, 143
Dickens, Charles, 30, 138
Dippity-Do, 95
Direct Mail, 22, 26, 64, 100, 137, 138–40, 142, 156, 177, 184. *See also* Promotion
Direct Marketing Association, 22, 137
Discounting, 20, 56, 59, 67, 77–78, 82, 90, 91, 97, 106, 126, 140, 144, 169, 172, 175–76. *See also* Pricing
Distribution, ix, 1, 10, 11, 13, 16, 17, 18, 21, 26, 53, 56, 61, 64, 73, 76, 77, 83, 86, 97, 100, 106, 112, 123, 125, 126–28, 130, 140, 148, 191
DKNY, 41
Doc Martens Shoes, 39
Doonan, Simon, 70–71
"Doonesbury," 148, 158
The Doors, 37
Door Store, 16
Dot Zero, 147
Drexler, Millard S. (Mickey), 67, 71
Dreyfuss, Richard, 81
Duany, Andres, 42
Du Pont, 152, 185
Duracell, 158

E

The Eagles, 39
Earth Day, 8
Earthsake, 182, 183
Eastman Kodak, 171
Eber, Jose, 95
Ed Debevic's Restaurant, 39, 133
Edward Scissorhands, 37
Egide, Mark, 180
Electronics, 43, 52–54, 104, 105, 109, 116, 117, 155
The Elephant Man, 21
Elle, 43, 59–61
Emma Peel, 81
Empire Diner, 161
Emporio Armani, 37, 119, 140

English Range Rover, 143
Enquirer, 59
Environmental Research Associates, 182
Equifax, 137
Eraserhead, 21
Esmark Apparel, 134
Esprit, 35, 184
Estée Lauder Inc., 10–11, 35, 108, 160, 163
Eureka Brewing Company, 109–10
Eureka Restaurant, 17–18, 22
Evans, Jane, 96
Events Marketing, 78, 171, 174
Eveready Battery Company, 158
Evian, 34, 56, 160
Excalibur Inc., 96

F

Fabergé, 73, 167
The Face, 37, 41, 161
Fads, vii, 28–29, 32, 42, 45, 55, 73, 74, 75, 78, 86, 87, 88, 90, 91, 96, 104, 149
Fame, 112
Family Circle, 59
F. A. O. Schwarz, 91
Farberware, Inc., 147
Fashion, 4, 5, 6, 11, 18, 20, 21, 26, 34–35, 37, 39, 42, 43, 44, 45–47, 48, 53–54, 59, 62, 63, 67–72, 92, 93, 94–95, 96–97, 104, 106, 109, 110, 111, 114, 115, 117, 119, 121, 122, 126, 128, 131, 134, 138, 139, 143, 144, 145, 147, 152, 155, 157, 161, 162, 164, 166, 169, 174, 175, 176, 181, 184, 185
Fatal Attraction, 160
The Fat Boys, 87
FCB/Leber Katz Partners, 29
Federal Express, 24
Ferrari Testarossa, 82
Fields, Patricia, 32, 33–34
Film, 5, 12, 15, 17, 21, 30, 31, 34, 81, 88, 109, 116, 140, 146, 151, 154, 160, 175
Filofax, 56
Financial Services, 12, 24, 25, 132, 135
Fincher, David, 32
Fisher, Donald G., 62, 67, 71, 104
Flamingo East Restaurant, 175
Flanders, Annie, 106
Flex Shampoo, 107
Fog City Diner, 39
Fonda, Jane, 30–31
Food, 18, 22, 26, 44, 74, 75, 76, 77, 79–80, 85, 104, 107, 108, 117, 121, 122, 126–27, 130, 142, 150, 151, 153, 155, 169, 175, 177, 180
Foote, Cone & Belding, 46
Foot Locker, 77
Forbes, Malcolm, 47
Ford Motor Company, 29, 42
Four Seasons Restaurant, 18, 122, 182
Fox, Michael J., 164
French's Mustard, 121
Friedman, Martin, 108
Fromm, Claude, 89
Fuji Film, 171

"Full House," 34

G

The Gap, 35, 43, 62, 63, 67-69, 70-71, 104, 106, 119, 122, 128, 155, 157, 162, 164, 166
Garcia, Jerry, 79
Garfield, Bob, 167
Garland, Judy, 135
Gaultier, Jean Paul, 161
Gehry, Frank, 112
General Electric, 141-42
General Mills, 96, 97, 109, 177
General Motors, 29, 184
Geoffrey Beene, 4
Georgette Klinger, 122
Gianni Versace, 39, 147
Gillette, 95
Gillette Sensor Razor, 121
Giorgio Armani, 6, 146. *See also* Emporio Armani
Giorgio of Beverly Hills, 26
Givenchy Hosiery, 134
Glaciér, 39, 40
Glenfiddich, 143
Goodman, John, 81
Gorman's New Product News, 108
Gotcha Sportswear, 117
The Gotham Restaurant, 6
Grand Metropolitan PLC, 66
Grange, Jacques, 33
Granita Restaurant, 22
Grant, Amy, 51
The Grateful Dead, 37, 79
Graves, Michael, 71, 117, 118
Great Bear, 109
Green Card, 146
Green Cross, 183
Greene, Gael, 129, 149
Greenfield, Jerry, 22, 79
Greeniaus, H. John, 107, 108
Green Marketing, 84, 101-2, 157, 179-85
Green Seal, 183
Greif, Paula, 35
Grey Poupon Mustard, 117, 121, 126-27
Guess Jeans, 37, 106
Guttenberg, Steve, 164

H

Häagen Dazs, 79
Haas, Robert, 46
Hachette Publications, 59
Hall, Arsenio, 164
Hall, Robert, 81, 85, 117
Hal's Restaurant, 130
Halston, 94, 110, 111
Hamilton, Bill, 35, 157
Hammer, MC, 37, 39, 164
Hanes Hosiery, 35
Hard Rock Cafe, 26, 184
Haring, Keith, 33, 37

Harley-Davidson, viii, 18, 21, 43, 47-48, 53-54, 82, 104, 119, 126, 155
Harris Poll, 137
Harry, Debbie, 94
Hart, Gary, 166
Hatfield, Tinker, 77, 116-17
Hatfield, Tucker, 85
Hawkins, Ansell, 55
Hayden, Tom, 30
Head & Shoulders, 109
Healthy Companies, Inc., 151
Hearst, Patty, 94
Hearst Magazines, 112, 144
Heinz Vinegar, 181
Hell's Angels, 48, 54
Hemingway, Ernest, 117, 158
Henri Bendel, 20, 114
Henry IV, Parts 1 and 2, 175
Herman, Pee-Wee, 147
Heublein, 174
HG, 143, 147
Hill, Holliday, Connors, Cosmopulos, 35
Holistic Health, 29, 56, 179
Hollywood Brat Packers, 47
Home Shopping Network, 141
Honda, 167
Hostess Twinkies, 74
Hotels, 12, 33, 39, 41, 94, 116, 117, 119, 122, 123, 136, 143, 147-48, 160, 182
Hoving, Thomas, 112, 132
Hoving, Walter, 114
Hudson's, 125
Hunter, Holly, 81

I

Iacocca, Lee, 158
Ice, Vanilla, 164
i-D, 37
Impact, 65, 87
Indochine Restaurant, 149, 175
Infiniti Cars, 35
Interior Design, 17, 39, 119, 122. *See also* Visual Design
International Events Group, 174
International Licensing Industry Merchandisers Association, 110
Interview, 67, 71, 112
Intimate Apparel Council, 152
Isozake, Arata, 33
Issey Miyake, 70
Isuzu, 167
Izod Lacoste, 44, 92, 96-97, 109, 126, 169

J

Jackson, Bo, 164
Jackson, Michael, 80, 164
Jagger, Mick, 58, 94
Jane's Addiction, 152
Jardine Fleming Securities, 109
Java Beans Coffeehouse, 130

J. C. Penney, 110, 111, 175
J. Crew, 139
J. D. Power & Associates, 158
Jean Paul Gaultier, 31
Jeep Cherokee, 30
Jello, 74
Jhirmack, 181
Jim Beam Kentucky Straight Bourbon
   Whiskey, 162
Johnson, Brad, 81
Johnson, Don, 164
Johnson & Johnson, 171, 181
John's Pizzeria, 114
Jordan, Michael, 78, 164, 165
Joseph E. Seagram & Sons Company, 151, 152
Judith Leiber, 153
J. Walter Thompson, 180

K

Kafka, Barbara, 41
Kahlo, Frida, 32
Kamikaze, 95
Katherine Hamnett, 161
Katz, Jon, 165, 166
Katzenberg, Jeffrey, 146
Keeble Duka Cavillo, 94
Kelley, Kitty, 148
Kellogg's Corn Flakes, 18, 44, 74
Kennedy, Caroline, 147
Kennedy, John, Jr., 4
Kerouac, Jack, 160
Kiam, Victor, 164
Kilgour French & Stanbury, 70
Kimberly Clark, 122
King, Stephen, 51
Kitsch, 122
Kleenex, 55
Klein, Calvin, 21, 39, 145, 146, 158
Klensch, Elsa, 35, 36
Knight, Philip, 75–76, 104
Knoll Group, 16
Kohler, 117
Kopelman, Arie L., 65, 108
Kotex, 122
Kraft, Neil, 32, 34–35, 71
Krier, Kevin, 136
Krups, 121

L

Lacoste, Rene, 96
Lacroix, Christian. *See* Christian Lacroix
L.A. Eyeworks, 113
Lagerfeld, Karl, 31, 62, 63–64, 70–71, 117, 143, 147
Lancôme, 16, 165
Landry, Tom, 51
Lane Bryant, 20
Langer, Andrew, 127
Lark Cigarettes, 154
Lattin, James, 170

Lauren, Ralph. *See* Ralph Lauren
Le Cirque Restaurant, 153
Leibovitz, Annie, 35, 49, 51
Le Madri Restaurant, 173
Lempert, Phil, 108
Lempert Report, 108
Lerner's, 20
Les Miserables, 149
Les Négresses Vertes, 135
Lettuce Entertain You Enterprises, 133
Levi Jeans, 18, 21, 43, 45–47, 48, 53–54, 67, 96, 117, 119, 152
Levin, Robert, 146
Levine, Carl, 121
Lewis, Richard, 65
License to Kill, 154
The Licensing Letter, 110
Like a Prayer, 32
The Limited, 20
Lincoln Continental, 166–67
Lindt, 122
Lippert, Barbara, 165
Lipschitz, Ralph, 119
Live Bait Restaurant, 113
The Living Room Coffee House, 122
Livingstone, Jennie, 34
Liz Claiborne Hosiery, 161
Loehmann's, 4
Loews Theaters, 134
Lopata, Sam, 119
Loquasto, Santo, 68
Lord & Taylor, 174
L'Oréal, 16, 59
Los Angeles, 143
Los Angeles County Museum of Art, 146. *See also* The Arts
Louis Vuitton Moet Hennessey, 127
Love, Gael, 112
Lox Around the Clock Restaurant, 119, 120
Luongo, Pino, 172–73
Lynch, David, 21, 145
Lyne, Adrian, 160
Lyon, J. B., 175

M

MAC, 143, 183
McCabe, Ed, 74, 143, 163
McCabe, George, 80
McDermott, Ian, 91
McDonald's, 39, 180
MacDowell, Andie, 146
McElligott Wright Morrison White, 76
Mackintosh, Cameron, 149
McLaren, Malcolm, 114
McNally, Brian, 149
Macy's, 94
Madonna, 30, 31–32, 34, 39, 58, 94, 114, 143, 147, 148, 164
Mail Preference Service, 22, 137
Manhattan School of Music, 66. *See also* The Arts
Mannering, Fred, 160

Marciano, Paul, 106
Mare Chiaro, 89
Marino, Peter, 70, 119
Marion's Continental Restaurant and Lounge, 122-23
Market Research, 52, 105, 176
Market Research Corporation, 176
Market Watch, 65
Mark Fox, 46
Marlboro Cigarettes, 21, 44, 73, 74, 119, 143
Marschalk Advertising, 127
MasterCard, 48, 50
Maxwell House Coffee, 121
Maybelline, 59
Mazar, Debi, 136
Mazda, 160
Mazda Miata, 44, 75, 77, 80-82, 85, 105, 116, 117, 155
Mazor, Boaz, 144
Mea Culpa, 143
Media Planning, 35-37, 66-67, 144-45, 146-49, 167-68
Mehle, Aileen ("Suzy"), 144
Mellencamp, John Cougar, 58, 169
Melman, Richard, 133
Meola, Peter, 152
Mercedes-Benz, 30
Merchandising/Display, 11, 13, 17, 26, 59-60, 64, 72, 83, 84, 92, 94, 100, 112, 116, 122, 123, 124, 128, 157
Metropolitan Home, 41, 71, 147
Metropolitan Museum of Art, 6, 112, 132, 134. See also The Arts
Michelob Beer, 152
Midler, Bette, 165
Mill Creek Natural Products, 180
Millenium, 147
Miller, Bryan, 173
Miller's Crossing, 140
Milliot, James, 148
Milton Bradley, 91
Minnelli, Liza, 74, 143
Mirabella, 60
Mirabella, Grace, 60
Miss Saigon, 149
Mitchell, Paul, 18
Moet & Chandon, 152
Mondino, Jean-Baptiste, 32
Monroe, Marilyn, 31, 46
Monsanto, 150
Montana, Claude, 143
Montana, Joe, 164
Moore, Demi, 164
Morgan Hotel Group, 33, 39, 116, 123
Morris, Bernadine, 64
Morris, William, 122
Morrison, Jim, 94
Morton's Restaurant, 146
Mother Teresa, 84
Mottus, Allan, 127
Mr. Coffee, 121
MTV, 31, 43, 57-59, 60-61, 87, 116, 169, 178, 184

Mudd Club, 136
Mueslix, 180
Museum of Modern Art, 35. See also The Arts
Music, 6, 8, 13, 28, 31, 35, 37, 39, 46, 57-59, 66, 87-88, 109, 135, 141, 159
Musto, Michael, 104-5, 113, 135
Muzak, 135

N

Nabisco Brands, 107, 108
Nagai, Peter, 95
Nancy Reagan, the Unauthorized Biography, 148
Nathan's Famous, 178
NBC, 147
Neiman Marcus, 50, 125
Neimark, Ira, 63
Netherland Hotel, 41
New Business Introductions, 1, 10, 11, 16-17, 24-25, 26, 52, 53, 63, 72, 86, 101, 104, 107-8, 119, 126, 127-28, 146-49, 156, 171
Newhall, Edith, 138
Newhouse, Si, 106
New Kids on the Block, 164
Newman, Paul, 51
News Cafe, 41
Newsweek, 15, 41, 133, 148
Newton, Helmut, 143
New York, 129, 138, 143, 149
New York City Ballet, 151. See also The Arts
The New Yorker, 15, 42, 143, 167
New York Philharmonic, 152. See also The Arts
The New York Post, 94, 147, 149
New York Shakespeare Festival, 35. See also The Arts
The New York Times, 28, 33, 41, 42, 60, 64, 143, 148, 148, 165, 173
Next Directory, 138
Niche Marketing, 52-53, 72, 81, 93, 104, 163
Nicholson, Jack, 143
Nickelodeon/Nick at Nite, 178, 184
Nielsen, Leslie, 164
Night Clubs, 18, 32, 37, 94, 113, 135, 146, 149, 152
Nike, 21, 35, 37, 44, 75-76, 77-79, 78, 85, 104, 106, 116-17, 121, 126, 128, 130, 152, 155, 159, 163, 165
9-1/2 Weeks, 160
Nissan, 80, 160
Nordstrom, 11, 111-12, 131
Norma Kamali, 41
Norwich, Billy, 149
Nozoe, Yuki, 52
NYNEX, 162

O

Oatmeal Crisp/Oatmeal Raisin Crisp Cereal, 177
Obsession (Fragrance), 21, 39, 145, 158

o.b. Tampons, 181
Odeon Restaurant, 55, 149
Ogilvy, David, 159
Ogilvy & Mather, 35, 157, 159
Ogilvy Center for Research and Development, 162
Old Spice After Shave, 73, 74
Olive Restaurant, 114
O'Malley, Kevin, 147
150 Wooster Restaurant, 149
O'Neill, Tip, 51
Oreo Cookies, 107
Origins Natural Resources, 5, 10-11, 108, 184-85
Orzechowski, Witold, 148
Oscar de la Renta, 144
Ozark, 109

P

Paglia, Camille, 31
Palazzetti, 16
Pali Arts Communications, 184
The Palladium, 32, 37
Palma, Laurie, 65
Pampers, 113
Pantene, 109
Panter, Gary, 147
Paper, 15, 33, 37, 38, 143, 144, 147
Papp, Joseph, 35
The Paramount Hotel, 33, 117, 119, 136, 147-48, 160
Pareles, Jon, 28, 165
Paris is Burning, 34
Parliament Lights Cigarettes, 162
Patagonia, Inc., 181
Patano, Patricia A., 158
Paterson, James H., 126
Patricia Field Boutique, 33-34
PBS, 168
People, 148
Pepin, Jacques, 147
Pepsi-Cola, 18, 37, 156, 164, 164-65, 172, 175
Perrier, 17, 43, 55-56, 60-61, 73, 108-9, 116, 117, 119, 126, 152, 155, 177
Perry Ellis, 39
Personal Products Corporation, 181
Pert Plus, 109
Peter Rogers Associates, 59
Petterson, Eric, 113
The Phantom of the Opera, 149
The Philadelphia Story, 88
Philanthropy. *See* Corporate Philanthropy
Philip Morris, 151, 154
Phillips, Julia, 95
Phillips, Lawrence S., 176
Phillips-Van Heusen Corporation, 176
Picasso, Paloma, 22, 23, 71, 145, 164
Pig Heaven Restaurant, 119
Plater-Zyberk, Elizabeth, 42
Playtex Family Products Corporation, 181
Plummer, Joe, 170
Poland Spring, 109

Porizkova, Paulina, 35
Porsche, 121
Positioning/Identity, 8-9, 11, 17, 18, 19-22, 25, 36, 46, 47, 48, 50-51, 53, 55, 60, 62-72, 77, 78, 79, 81, 83, 88, 97, 99, 100, 101, 103, 104, 106, 107, 108, 110, 111, 112, 117, 119, 123, 126, 128, 130, 132, 135, 139, 150, 152, 155, 156, 157, 158, 160, 161, 162-67, 168, 170, 172, 174, 177, 178, 180, 182, 187, 188, 190, 192, 193
Postrio Restaurant, 22
Premiums, 16, 20, 24, 59-60, 83, 101, 113, 140, 169, 170, 172, 177-78
Prescriptives, 10, 108
Pressman, Gene, 70
Pricing, 21, 33, 50, 52-53, 67, 92, 95, 100, 112-13, 170, 175-76, 190-91. *See also* Discounting
Princess Diana, 84
Private Eye, 89
Procter & Gamble, 73, 109, 113, 163, 177, 180, 183, 184
Promotion, ix, vii, viii, 1, 11, 15, 17, 24, 26, 56, 58, 78, 92, 100, 101, 102, 112, 113, 169-78, 182-85, 192. *See also* Direct Mail; Public Relations
Psychedelia, 37
Psychographics, ix, 9, 99, 105
Public Relations, ix, viii, 25, 26, 53, 71, 77, 100, 101, 105, 112, 143-54, 191. *See also* Promotion
Publishers Clearing House, 138
Publishing, 59-61, 88-89, 110, 148
Puck, Wolfgang, 17-18, 22, 106, 108, 109-10
Purchase Behavior, viii, 1, 9, 14-27, 29, 92, 93, 101, 103, 122, 128, 137, 155-56, 164, 169
Putnam, Andree, 33

Q

Quaker Oats Squares, 153
Quinn, Jane Bryant, 15

R

Radical Chic, 30
Radio, 168
Rafferty, Terrence, 15
Raleigh Hotel, 41
Ralph Lauren, 39, 46, 96, 119, 135
Ray Bans Wayfarer, 154
Reagan, Nancy, 71, 89, 148
Rechelbacher, Horst, 8
Red Cross, 176
Reebok International, 78, 78, 162
Reflexology, 182
Reiki, 179
Reiss, Spencer, 41
Remington, 164
"Remote Control," 59
Restaurant News, 36, 147

Restaurants, 6, 17–18, 22, 26, 39, 41, 55, 89, 108, 113, 114, 119, 120, 122–23, 125, 127, 130, 133, 146, 149, 152, 153, 161, 173, 175, 180, 182, 184
Revlon Inc., 107
"Revolution," 35
Rice, Donna, 166
Risky Business, 154
Ritts, Herb, 68
The Ritz (Nightclub), 94, 152
Ritz Bar, 18
Rivera, Diego, 32
Rivers, Larry, 68, 71
Road & Track, 82
Roberti, William V., 176
Roberts, Julia, 46
Rockbill, 165
Rockenwagner Restaurant, 130
The Rocketeer, 175
Rock Hotel, 94
Roddick, Anita, 83–84, 150
Rogers, Mike, 75, 87
Rolex, 56
Rolling Stone, 161, 162
Romeo Gigli Boutique, 114, 115
Roper Poll, 131
"Roseanne," 153
Rosen, Bob, 151
Ross, Lee Radziwell, 146
Rossellini, Isabella, 165
Roux, Michel, 62–63, 66–67, 71, 104
The Royalton Hotel, 33, 39, 41, 117
R. T. French Company, 127
Rubell, Steve, 32
Russell, Mary, 41
Russian Tea Room, 152

S

Saatch, Charles, 89
Saban, Stephen, 41, 42
¡Sabroso¡ Restaurant, 130
Saks Fifth Avenue, 70, 125
Salik, Norman, 154
Saltzman, Elizabeth, 94
Saltzman, Ellin, 94
Sann, Tedd, 164
San Pellegrino, 56
Savage, Fred, 164
Scattergories, 91
Scharf, Kenny, 33, 66
Schlossberg, Edwin, 147
Schrager, Ian, 32–33, 37, 106, 136, 147, 182
Schroff, Peter, 117
Schulhof, Michael, 109
Scott, John, 180
Scully, Vincent, 42
The Sculpture Gardens Restaurant, 130
Sears, 77, 92–93
Secret Deodorant, 183
Selchow & Righter, 90, 91
Sellars, Peter, 166

Semiotics, ix, 17, 20, 37, 99–100, 103, 111–15, 152, 155, 160
The Seventh Generation, 5
Sevres, 167
sex, lies and videotape, 5, 146
The Sex Pistols, 94
Shabby Chic, 121
Shepherd, Cybill, 164
Shiatsu, 17
Shoemaker, Willie, 49
Shriner, Richard, 88
Simmons Market Research, 52
Simon & Schuster, 148
Sinatra, Frank, 152
"Sixty Minutes," 168
SMH, 88
Smith, Liz, 89, 144
Smith, Michael, 170
Snickers, 122
Snow, Phoebe, 165
Soho Training Center, 136
Solomon, Michael, 132
Solters, Lee, 166
Sondheim, Stephen, 51
Sony, 43, 52–54, 104, 105, 109, 116, 117, 155
Sound Factory, 113
Spago Restaurant, 22, 108
Sperry Top-Sider, 178
Spielberg, Stephen, 81
Spin, 41
Spokespersons, 51, 101, 162, 163, 164–66
Sprouse, Stephen, 44, 92, 94–95, 97
Spy, 44, 86, 88–89, 91, 171
Starck, Philippe, 33, 39, 40, 117, 147
Stephens Inc., 176
Stephen Sprouse. *See* Sprouse, Stephen
Steuben, 117, 118, 172
Stewart, Jimmy, 88
Stewart, Scott, 113
Sting, 58
Stolichnaya, 143
Stone, Oliver, 5
Streep, Meryl, 51, 143
Studio 54, 32
Stutz, Geraldine, 20, 114
The Sun Also Rises, 158
Sure Deodorant, 183
Surfrider Foundation, 185
Swatch Watch, 37, 44, 86, 87–88, 91, 119, 152
Sweepstakes, 20, 24, 101, 138, 178

T

Taco Bell, 39
Tai Chi, 182
Tattoos, 37, 47
Taylor, Elizabeth, 148
Taylor, N. Powell, 141–42
TBWA, Inc., 21, 63, 65, 89, 157, 161
Teiger, David, 132
Telemarketing, 22, 101, 137, 140–42
Telephone Preference Service, 137

Television, 5, 21, 22, 31, 35–36, 51, 54, 57–59, 69, 77, 127, 141, 152, 157, 158, 168, 171, 174, 184
Tenax, 44, 92, 95–96, 97, 107
Terre Verde Trading Company, 182
Thackeray, William Makepeace, 30
Thatcher, Margaret, 89
Thomas English Muffins, 26
Thompson, Jan, 81
The Thompson Twins, 88
Tide Detergent, 177
Tiffany & Company, 22, 109, 114, 139, 145, 146
Timberland Shoes, 30
Time, 66–67, 148
The Time Cafe, 182
Timex, 35
The Toasters, 152
"Today Show," 147
Todd Oldham Fashion Show, 145
Toyota, 29, 151, 160, 184
Transportation, viii, 18, 21, 29, 30, 35, 42, 43, 44, 47–48, 53–54, 56, 75, 77, 80–82, 85, 104, 105, 116, 117, 119, 121, 126, 143, 151, 155, 155, 158, 160, 167, 184
Travel, 7, 8, 11, 12, 17, 24, 26, 41, 132, 148–49, 172. *See also* American Express; Club Med
Trends, Forecasting, vii, 10, 28–42
Triumph Spitfire, 81
Trivial Pursuit, 28–29, 44, 90–91, 126
Trudeau, Garry, 148, 158
The Tunnel, 89
Turner, Ted, 31
TV Guide, 59
Twentieth Century Fox Film Corporation, 140
21 Club, 146
"Twin Peaks," 21
Tyson, Mike, 164

U

Uncle Dave's Kitchen, 175
United Brands International, 175
United Research, 132
USA Today, 89
US Magazine, 39
U.S. Travel Data Center, 181
Utne Reader, 37, 184

V

Vadhera, Dave, 165
Vadim, Roger, 30
Valentino, 135
Vanderbilt, Cornelius, 117
Vanity Fair, 5, 22, 33, 143, 145, 146, 147, 168
Varnedoe, Kirk, 35
Versace, Gianni. *See* Gianni Versace
Vicious, Sid, 94
Victoria's Secret, 20, 138
Vidal Sassoon, 109

Video Storyboard Tests, Inc., 161, 165
Village Voice, 105, 113, 147
Vince & Eddie's Restaurant, 119
Visa, 48, 50, 172
Visual Design, ix, 72, 100, 116–24, 138. *See also* Interior Design
Vivian Westwood, 26
Vogue, 34, 42, 59, 67, 71, 94, 143, 144, 147
"Vogueing," 33–34
Volvo, 143
Vons Supermarket, 26
Vreeland, Diana, 131

W

W, 41, 143, 147
Waldock, Michael, 123
Walker, Daniel E., 68
Wall Street, 5
The Wall Street Journal, 34, 147
Wal-Mart, 93
Walt Disney Company, 110, 112, 132, 146, 175
Walters, Frank, 65
Warhol, Andy, 63, 66, 71, 94
Warwick Baker & Fiore, 141
Wayne, George, 15, 33, 144
Weber, Bruce, 21, 39, 147
Weiden, Dan, 159
Weiden & Kennedy, 21, 35, 78, 159
Weill, Kurt, 159
Weir, Peter, 146
Wells, Linda, 144
Wendy's, 127
Wertheimer, Alain, 62, 63, 70–71
Whyte, William, 176
The Wild One, 47
Wilhemina, 42
Willis, Bruce, 164
Willis & Geiger, 117
Will You Please Be Quiet, Please?, 143
Winston, Clifford, 160
Wintour, Anna, 60, 147
Wolfe, Tom, 30, 179
The Women, 5
Women's Wear Daily, 29, 36, 63, 147, 148
Wright, Tony, 76–77

Y

Yamaha, 108
Yamamoto, Kenichi, 81
Yoga, 182
Yohji Yamamoti, 41
You'll Never Eat Lunch in this Town Again, 95
Young MC, 39

Z

Zoli, 42

Other Business One Irwin Titles of Interest to You

Megabrands: How to Build Them, How to Beat Them
John Loden

Shows you how to leverage the strength of a brand leader and build market share, customer loyalty, and sales. Using schematics and visual aids, author Loden helps you identify your strengths and your competition's weaknesses. Market leaders can discover where the best opportunities for leveraging exist. Competing brands can locate and dominate profitable market niches.

ISBN: 1-55623-469-4 $27.50

The Complete Guide to Regional Marketing
Shawn McKenna

The first comprehensive look at promotion, advertising, and pricing strategies for regional marketing. McKenna details how to create a principled blueprint for assessing and developing sales and marketing plans by following the Marketing Assessment Process (MAP). Using *The Complete Guide to Regional Marketing*, you can develop regional brand strategies, "customer-ize" your marketing efforts, and surpass the competitive challenges you face.

ISBN: 1-55623-422-8 $27.50

Creating Demand: Powerful Tips and Tactics for Marketing Your Product or Service
Richard Ott

Richard Ott goes way beyond the "4 Ps" and explains the real demand building process. He shows you how to set the stage for success, how to leverage demand to peak levels, and how to sustain it. He explains how person-to-person human influence actually works, and how you can tap into the tremendous power of human influence to affect the masses—and cause demand to erupt!

ISBN: 1-55623-560-7 $27.50

Selling to the Affluent: The Professional's Guide to Closing the Sales that Count
Dr. Thomas Stanley

Improve your closing percentage ... and income. Stanley shows you how to approach wealthy prospects at the moment they are most likely to buy. In *Marketing to the Affluent* Stanley told you how to find them. Now he tells you how to sell them.

ISBN: 1-55623-418-X $55.00

Niche Selling: How to Find Your Customer in a Crowded Market
Bill Brooks

In his practical, straightforward approach, Brooks directs you through the entire niche selling process. He shows you how to develop workable sales strategies based on customer loyalty, prestige, referrals, and alliances. Discover how to enhance your standing in the minds of prospects and customers using the power of personal positioning.

ISBN: 1-55623-499-6 $24.95

Prices Quoted in U.S. Currency and are Subject to Change Without Notice. Available in Fine Bookstores and Libraries Everywhere.